LB160
Professional communication skills for business studies

The Open U

Book **2** | # Writing
Successful
Essays

Prepared for the course team by Jim Donohue,
Lina Adinolfi, Derek Davies and Prithvi Shrestha

This publication forms part of an Open University course LB160 *Professional communication skills for business studies*. Details of this and other Open University courses can be obtained from the Student Registration and Enquiry Service, The Open University, PO Box 197, Milton Keynes MK7 6BJ, United Kingdom: tel. +44 (0)845 300 60 90, email general-enquiries@open.ac.uk

Alternatively, you may visit the Open University website at www.open.ac.uk where you can learn more about the wide range of courses and packs offered at all levels by The Open University.

To purchase a selection of Open University course materials visit www.ouw.co.uk, or contact Open University Worldwide, Michael Young Building, Walton Hall, Milton Keynes MK7 6AA, United Kingdom for a brochure. tel. +44 (0)1908 858793; fax +44 (0)1908 858787; email ouw-customer-services@open.ac.uk

The Open University

Walton Hall, Milton Keynes

MK7 6AA

First published 2008. Second edition 2009

Edited and designed by The Open University.

Typeset by Pam Callow, S&P Enterprises Ltd, Lydbrook, Glos. GL179PP

Printed in the United Kingdom by Cambrian Printers, Aberystwyth

ISBN 978 0 7492 2542 1

2.1

The paper used in this publication contains pulp sourced from forests independently certified to the Forest Stewardship Council (FSC) principles and criteria. Chain of custody certification allows the pulp from these forests to be tracked to the end use. (see www.fsc-uk.org).

FSC

Mixed Sources

Product group from well-managed forests and other controlled sources

Cert no. TT-COC-2200
www.fsc.org
© 1996 Forest Stewardship Council

Contents

5

The course team

Lina Adinolfi (author)

Haider Ali (OU Business School adviser)

Liz Benali (course manager)

Jim Donohue (course team chair)

Elizabeth J. Erling (course team member)

Helen Peters (author)

Prithvi Shrestha (author)

Production team

Mandy Anton (graphic designer)

Ann Carter (print buyer)

Peter Lee (editor)

Jon Owen (graphic artist)

Simon Rodwell (media project manager)

Amanda Smith (editor)

Nikki Tolcher (media assistant)

Consultant authors

Derek Davies (University of Manchester)

David Lewis (DML Communication Services, The Netherlands)

External assessor

George Blue (University of Southampton)

Critical readers

Olwyn Alexander (Heriot-Watt University)

Dennis Beer (B200 tutor)

David Hann (E301 and E303 tutor)

Malcolm Harris (B200 tutor)

Mary Lewis (B200 tutor)

Peter Martin (B200 tutor)

Brian Terry (B200 tutor)

Geraldine Wooley (B200 tutor)

We would like to thank the following former B200 students for their contribution to the course design:

Dimitri Billaud

Vera Brenner

Carmen Jaffke

Klaus Konwalin

Gareth Price

Jitendra Ranpura

Caroline Siddall

Tibebu Tefeta

Thanks also go to the following business school students for giving us permission to use their assignments as examples of good practice:

Wayne Barker

Anne Buckingham

Rebecca Britain

Rebecca Chadwick

Assumpta Corley

Lee Farndon

Nicola Fink

Stephanie Firth

Jenny Frister

Ruth Fulton

Rupert Groves

Claire Houlden

Emma Kingston

Tom Laverick

John Lyons

Daniel McCarthy

Nicola McKee

Damian Millington

Ian Pegg

Noel Rafferty

David Sharp

Yoshie Shinoyama

Jenny Sprackling

Martin Surrey

Angela Temple

Christine Thomas

Amanda Todd

Pamela Vang

Debbie Walker

SESSION **1 What is an essay?**

1.1 Introduction

The world of business studies is a world of texts. Case studies, course textbooks, company reports, newspaper articles, websites and financial statements are the texts which make up that world. But one type of text is different: **essays**.

Essays are different because of who writes them and why they are written. They are written exclusively by students and they are written as a way of learning about an aspect of business or for assessment purposes. However, although they are written for these study purposes, the skills involved are professional communication skills.

The essence of successful professional communication is the ability to adapt your writing to a particular situation, task and audience. Learning to succeed at essay writing is a valuable opportunity to develop this ability. Through the processes of researching, designing and producing a university-level essay, you will enhance the skills that ensure success in workplace communication generally.

Learning outcomes

In this session you will:

- compare extracts from three texts: an essay, a company website presentation, and an online discussion
- look at some differences between writing an essay and speaking
- learn about the four aspects that tutors look for when they read an essay: relevance, argument, source material and presentation
- study what 'argument' means in an essay
- begin to study academic language.

1.2   What are essays like?

Essays are texts. They consist mostly of words, organised in particular ways to fulfil particular purposes in particular situations. Case studies, course textbooks, company reports, newspaper articles, websites and financial statements are also texts but they are organised in different ways to fulfil different purposes in different situations and some of them do not consist of words alone.

In the first activity you will compare a short extract from an essay with two other contrasting texts.

Activity 1.1

Purpose: to match three extracts with the texts they come from.

Task: look at Extracts 1.1, 1.2 and 1.3 in Resource Book 2. Each one is from one of the text-types listed in the right-hand column below. Decide which text each extract comes from and indicate this by drawing a line between the extract and the text type below. When you have finished, note down one or two features of each extract which you used to make your decision.

Extract	Text type
1.1	Sports-shoe discussion website
1.2	Business studies essay
1.3	Company website

Compare your answers with those suggested in the Answer section.

Comment

You can often tell quite easily what kind of text a short extract comes from because different types of text have particular design features. The skills of recognising and using these design features are professional communication skills. The next activity looks more closely at some of the features of the three extracts.

Activity 1.2

Purpose: to focus on the knowledge that you used to identify Extracts 1.1 to 1.3.

Task: in this activity use the letters CW to refer to the Nike company website; E to refer to the student's essay; and SS to refer to the sports-shoe discussion website.

The six scales below grade some distinctive features of texts. Use these scales to compare the three text types. For example, if you think the student's essay is very formal, write 'E' in the box at the right-hand end of the scale. If you think it is very informal, write E in the box at the left-hand end. If you think it is neither very formal nor very informal, write E in the middle box of the scale. This first one is done for you as an example. Do you agree that it belongs there? Where would you place the Nike and the sports shoe discussion websites on this scale?

Don't worry if you are unsure what some of the features mean. They are explained in detail in the Answer section.

Informal   Formal

				E

Personal   Impersonal

Everyday style/non-specialist   Technical/specialist

Easy to read   Difficult to read

Loosely organised text   Strongly organised text

More speech-like   More writing-like

Compare your answers with those suggested in the Answer section.

Comment

Extracts 1.1 to 1.3 are very generally about the same topic – sports shoes – but they deal with this subject differently. If you had the whole texts, you would see the differences in their **content**, **organisation** and **language** even more clearly. The reason their content, organisation and language differ is that the **purposes**, **writers** and **readers** of each text are distinct.

The next activity looks more closely at these distinct purposes, writers and readers.

Activity 1.3

Purpose: to identify the purposes, writers and readers of Extracts 1.1 to 1.3.

Task: the tables below list some possible text purposes, readers and writers. Tick the most likely purposes, readers and writers for the text each extract comes from. An example is given to get you started.

	Extract 1.1	Extract 1.2	Extract 1.3
Why was the text written?			
To give a detailed history of the company	☐	☐	☐
For entertainment	☐	☐	☐
To create a good impression of Nike	✓	☐	☐
To explain why Nike is the largest sports and fitness company in the world	☐	☐	☐
To review a new trainer design	☐	☐	☐
To learn about company performance in the modern business world	☐	☐	☐
Who is the writer?			
A friend of the reader's	☐	☐	☐
A company analyst	☐	☐	☐
A friend of Bill Bowerman	☐	☐	☐
An athlete	☐	☐	☐
A public relations officer	☐	☐	☐
A student	☐	☐	☐
A tutor	☐	☐	☐
Who is the reader?			
The general public	☐	☐	☐
Sports shoe fans	☐	☐	☐
A tutor	☐	☐	☐
A student	☐	☐	☐
A company analyst	☐	☐	☐
A public relations officer	☐	☐	☐
Athletes	☐	☐	☐
A friend of the writer	☐	☐	☐

Compare your answers with those suggested in the Answer section.

Comment

To understand fully why essays are different, you need to come back to their purpose. Like all texts, one purpose of an essay is to communicate but, in reality, an essay writer is doing three things at the same time. They are communicating; they are learning; and, usually, they are being assessed. The next section will look more closely at how essay writers use their communication skills in order to learn and be assessed.

The last part of this section summarises some of the features that make an essay text different from other texts.

Spoken and written language

Spoken language and written language are quite different from each other. When people speak there is usually someone listening. The speaker receives feedback from their listener and adapts the language they use in response. As a result, spoken language can contain corrections, changes of direction, hesitations and contradictions. These are normal and do not usually interfere with communication. However, when people write there is more time to plan the language they use, review and correct it, and as a result written language is more concise and tightly organised than spoken language. Knowing the differences between spoken and written language is an important basis for successful communication.

As you saw in Activity 1.2, the distinction between a more **spoken** style and a more **written** style is helpful when analysing different text types. Before you read any further, look at the extracts below from two of the texts you have been reading about. Decide which is more written and which is more spoken and note down the reasons for your decision.

Extract A

The guy has a lot of hype around him and I've argued back and forth on NT about who the best player is but that is neither here nor there. I'm not on the bandwagon now but this is my feelings and opinion of this basketball shoe.

Extract B

Whilst studying at university, Knight's business skills were evident when he produced a paper citing the benefits of producing sports shoes in countries with cheaper labour than the USA (a policy now implemented by all major training shoe companies).

The table below focuses on what language features make Extract A seem more like speaking and Extract B more like writing.

More spoken style (Extract A)	More written style (Extract B)
Context-dependent (Here and now) This means a text focuses on what is happening at the time of speaking. It includes words such as *now*, *here*, *this*: not on the bandwagon *now*, *this* is my feeling, *this* shoe	**Context-independent (Not here, not now)** This means a text focuses on events that are not happening at the time of speaking. All the information has to be provided for the reader who is not in the situation. … a paper citing the benefits of producing sports shoes in countries with cheaper labour than the USA [not *this paper*]
Personal One feature that makes speech more personal is the use of first person pronouns: *I've* argued, *I'm* not, *my* feelings	**Impersonal** The opinions in the text are expressed impersonally. … business skills were evident [not *I think he had good business skills*]
Informal, colloquial, everyday language The *guy*, a lot of *hype* around him, not on the *bandwagon*	**Formal, specialist language** … a policy now implemented by all major training shoe companies [not *a lot of training shoe companies now use this way of working*]
Many, generally short, clauses joined by simple conjunctions In the examples below, the clauses are on different lines. The conjunctions are underlined. The guy has a lot of hype around him <u>and</u> I've argued back and forth on NT about who the best player is <u>but</u> that is neither here nor there	**Long noun groups, longer clauses, more complicated conjunctions** In the examples below, the clauses are on different lines, the conjunctions are underlined and the noun groups are boxed. Whilst studying at university Knight's business skills were evident <u>when</u> he produced a paper citing the benefits of producing sports shoes in countries with cheaper labour than the USA (a policy now implemented by all major training shoe companies).

Activity 1.4 ....

Purpose: to reinforce your knowledge of some differences between spoken and written language.

Task: look again through Extracts 1.1, 1.2 and 1.3 and find some examples of the following language features for each text.

More spoken style	*More written style*
Context-dependent (Here and now)	**Context-independent (Not here, not now)**
Extract 1.1 _____	Extract 1.1 _____
_____	_____
Extract 1.2 _____	Extract 1.2 _____
_____	_____
Extract 1.3 _____	Extract 1.3 _____
_____	_____
Personal	**Impersonal**
Extract 1.1 _____	Extract 1.1 _____
_____	_____
Extract 1.2 _____	Extract 1.2 _____
_____	_____
Extract 1.3 _____	Extract 1.3 _____
_____	_____
Informal, colloquial, everyday language	**Formal, specialised language**
Extract 1.1 _____	Extract 1.1 _____
_____	_____
Extract 1.2 _____	Extract 1.2 _____
_____	_____
Extract 1.3 _____	Extract 1.3 _____
_____	_____
Many, generally short, clauses joined by simple conjunctions	**Long noun groups, longer clauses, more complicated conjunctions**
Extract 1.1 _____	Extract 1.1 _____
_____	_____
Extract 1.2 _____	Extract 1.2 _____
_____	_____
Extract 1.3 _____	Extract 1.3 _____

Compare your answers with those suggested in the Answer section.

Comment

The language of the essay (Extract 1.3) is more written in style than that of either the company website or the sports shoe discussion website. As usual, the reason for the differences between these texts lies in their distinct purposes. The essay is intended to show the reader how the writer can discuss the assignment title they have been set. The company website is designed to project a positive image of Nike and appeal to the company's existing and potential customers. The text from the sports shoe website is probably a marketing tool, although it is designed to seem like an online chat room where sports fans share views about the latest training shoe.

In fact, all of these texts are written, including the sports shoe text. This shows that it is possible to write text **as if** it is spoken. However, a written text with these kinds of spoken features is not suitable for an essay. The next section looks more closely at the reason why.

1.3   What do tutors think a successful essay is like?

As with all written communication, success in essay writing depends on an awareness of your reader. In some ways a tutor is an unusual reader. Most readers read because they are interested in finding out new information about a topic. However, a tutor is unlikely to be so interested in learning new information about the topic of your essay. They are more interested in learning new information about *you*, the writer. They want to find out how you are thinking, what you are learning, and how you communicate your thinking and learning through your essay.

John Clanchy and Brigid Ballard, two university lecturers, analysed the comments of their colleagues on many students' essays. They identified the four main characteristics that tutors look for in an essay:

1   relevance to the essay title
2   a reasoned argument
3   use of source texts
4   appropriate presentation.

(Source: Clanchy and Ballard, 1998)

The four characteristics of a successful essay

1 Relevance to the essay title

Here are some examples of what tutors say:

Good work. You've covered the topic well and put much thought into your essay.

The second major fault in the essay is that far too much of it is not immediately relevant to the topic you chose. The task before you was quite specific and clear. Instead of tackling that task directly and without delay, you write around the topic for page after page. Why not go directly to the evidence ... asking yourself, 'What does this tell me in answer to the question before me?'

(Clanchy and Ballard, 1998, p. 5)

It is therefore important to be sure that you are clear about what the essay title requires of you.

Essay titles include some or all of the following parts:

*   an introductory statement about the topic
*   instruction words
*   key concepts
*   guidelines about the scope of the essay.

The activities in this session concentrate on the instruction words and key concepts in an essay title, as these will underpin your writing.

Instruction words in essay titles

Activity 1.5 ....

Purpose: to introduce some instruction words from essay titles.

Task: there are four examples of business studies essay titles below. Underline the instruction words in each title. You don't need to understand the concepts in the titles for this activity.

1   From your understanding of the organisational context for management, define the terms 'environment' and 'structure'.
2   Compare and contrast hard Human Resource Management approaches with soft ones.

3 Explain why Nike is the biggest training shoe company in the world.

4 Discuss how business processes might affect an organisation's ability to compete effectively.

Compare your answers with those suggested in the Answer section.

Comment

There are many possible instruction words, each requiring you to do something different in your essay. The next activity looks at a selection of these words. Although there are so many instruction words, you will see that essays can effectively be grouped into three main types.

Activity 1.6

Purpose: to introduce some instruction words used in essay titles.

Task: the three lists below contain mixed-up instruction words and their definitions. For each list, match the instruction words with their correct definition.

List 1

analyse	(a) Look for similarities and differences between the items under discussion.
compare	(b) Take apart an idea, a concept or a statement in order to consider all the factors it consists of. It should be very methodically and logically organised.
contrast	(c) Write about the main points of the information available on a subject and not the details.
summarise	(d) Look for differences between the items under discussion.

List 2

define	(a) Weigh up the arguments surrounding an issue, using your own opinions and, more importantly, reference to the work of other people.
describe	(b) Give reasons for and against; investigate and examine by argument.
discuss	(c) State precisely what is meant by a particular issue, theory or concept.
evaluate	(d) Give a detailed account of.

List 3

assess	(a) Make clear by the use of example.
illustrate	(b) Make something clear or give reasons for something.
explain	(c) Make comments about the value or importance of the concepts and ideas under discussion.

Compare your answers with those suggested in the Answer section.

Comment

Each instruction word asks for a different kind of essay. However, as mentioned above, it is possible to group all these essays into three main types. All the instruction words in this activity can be grouped under these three headings, as follows.

Type of essay	Instruction word	What the essay is about
Description	summarise define describe illustrate	What or how something is How two or more things are
Explanation	explain analyse	How something works How something influences something
Discussion	analyse discuss evaluate assess compare contrast	What people think about something

Here are the essay titles from Activity 1.5 grouped into these three main types.

Description essay

From your understanding of the organisational context for management, define the terms 'environment' and 'structure'.

Explanation essay

Explain why Nike is the biggest training shoe company in the world.

Discussion essay

Discuss how business processes might affect an organisation's ability to compete effectively.

Compare and contrast hard HRM approaches with soft ones.

University essays are often of the discussion type. **Discussion** essays usually require you to include some explanation and description as well. In this introductory session you will look at an **explanation** essay and in Sessions 2 to 6 you will work with **discussion** essays.

The four essay titles that you will work with in this book are as follows.

1   Explain why Nike is the biggest training shoe company in the world. (Session 1)

2   Discuss the extent to which a large corporation such as Nike might influence the economic health of a developing country. (Sessions 2 and 3)

3   Critically discuss why markets may fail to deliver socially desirable outcomes. (Session 4)

4   Wal-Mart is a USA-based multinational corporation. Critically discuss the likely costs and benefits of its takeover of Asda, a UK-based company. (Sessions 5 and 6)

Key concepts of essay titles

The instruction words tell you what to do. The **key concepts** tell you what to do this to. Some of the key concepts in business essay titles may be quite well-known concepts, such as *human resource management* or *investment*. Others, such as *value chain* or *critical success factors*, may be more specialised. Usually, key concepts are abstract nouns (a single word such as 'investment') or noun groups (several words in a group such as 'critical success factors'). You are expected to use these terms in the way they are understood in your business studies course.

The next activity focuses on the key concepts in five essay titles. For this activity, you don't need to understand what all the concepts mean.

Activity 1.7 ....

Purpose: to practise recognising key concepts.

Task: highlight all the key concepts in the essay titles below. Remember that a key concept may be a single noun or a noun group with several words in it.

1   From your understanding of the organisational context for management, define the terms 'environment' and 'structure'.

2   Compare and contrast hard Human Resource Management approaches with soft ones.

3   Explain Porter's concept of the Value Chain and comment on its implications for the design of organisations.

4   Explain why Nike is the biggest training shoe company in the world.

5   Discuss how business processes might affect an organisation's ability to compete effectively.

Compare your answers with those suggested in the Answer section.

Comment ....

Key concepts make up networks of knowledge in business studies. They can be drawn as **mind maps**.

Figure 1.1 shows the beginning of a mind map for the concept 'value chain' from a business studies course.

As you can see, there are several concepts around the key concept 'value chain'. It is possible to draw in other concepts as well. There

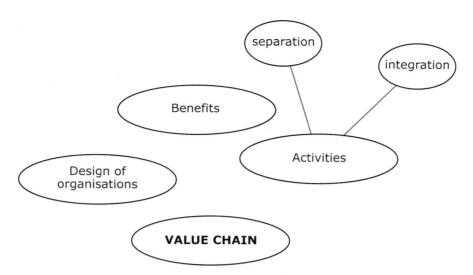

Figure 1.1   A mind map for the concept *value chain*

are links between three of the concepts – activities, separation and integration. These links are important. Often an essay title will tell you which concepts to link.

Activity 1.8

Purpose: to note how an essay title tells you to link concepts.

Task: here is the essay title about the value chain again:

Explain Porter's concept of the Value Chain and comment on its implications for the design of organisations.

Which two concepts are linked in this title? Draw the link on the mind map in Figure 1.1. Which words in the title indicate the link? Underline those words.

Compare your answers with those suggested in the Answer section.

Comment

It is important that you can recognise how the concepts in an essay title are linked. Very often you are being asked to write about this link in your essay.

Activity 1.9

Purpose: to practise further noting the links between the concepts in essay titles.

Task: look again at the list of essay titles in Activity 1.7 and underline the words which tell you how to link the concepts that you previously identified in them.

Compare your answers with those suggested in the Answer section.

Comment

Essay titles are sometimes called essay **questions** although, as you can see from the titles you have looked at, they are not actual questions. A good technique for seeing the links between the concepts in a title is, nevertheless, to turn the title into a question.

Activity 1.10 ....

Purpose: to check what an essay title expects you to do by turning it into a question.

Task: essay title 1 in Activity 1.7 can be turned into the following question:

From your understanding of the organisational context for management, what do the terms 'environment' and 'structure' mean?

Now rewrite essay titles 2 to 5 as questions.

Compare your answers with those suggested in the Answer section.

Comment ....

When you turn an essay title into a question, you can see more clearly what you are being asked to do. However, that is only the start. Tutors have certain expectations about **how** you go about responding to the task. The most important of these expectations is that you write an **argument**. The next section looks at the meaning of 'argument' in essay writing.

2 A reasoned argument

In everyday situations, an argument means two people in a conflict over a difference of opinion. It is something people often want to avoid.

In essay writing, your tutor **expects** arguments. Like everyday arguments, arguments in essays may be about differences of opinion. However, there is another meaning to the word 'argument'. Your tutor expects to see that your ideas fit together in a logical way.

Here are some tutors' comments about this.

This essay shows good understanding of the course and the issues it raises. It is also clearly structured and written.

You have covered the main points in a succinct way with a very focused essay. You also needed to have some more explanation of some of the points, so perhaps a little too focused.

A competent piece of work with a logical structure, including an effective introduction and a well considered, if lengthy, conclusion.

The essay introduction is a good place to begin to look at the meaning of argument in essay writing. Good essay introductions start an argument by linking back to the essay title and linking forward towards the essay itself.

Argument in essays – the introduction

Activity 1.11 ....

Purpose: to identify some features of a good essay introduction.

Task 1: read the student's essay introduction below in Extract C and decide how well you think it introduces the argument of the essay. Make some notes or underline any parts you think do this. Then do Task 2.

> ### Extract C
>
> ### *Explain why Nike is the biggest training shoe company in the world.*
>
> For a company to be regarded as the biggest in its business sector, it has to be successful. Nike is certainly a story of success. From its humble origins in the early 1970s to a 43% market share in the USA in 2005, the success of Nike has been built on two strategies: marketing and innovation. This essay will examine how the marketing strategy and the company mission 'to bring inspiration and innovation to every athlete in the world' (Nike website, 2005) have made the company into a leading brand throughout the world.

Task 2: the first column in the table below describes the words that contribute to a good introduction. In the blank column write down any words from the student's introduction above which you think are good examples of these.

Words that contribute to a good introduction	Examples
Words which link back to the title	
Words which identify the key concepts in the essay	
Words which state the central argument of the essay	
Words which say how the essay will be organised	

Compare your answers with those suggested in the Answer section.

Comment ....

Using words connected with the title, identifying key concepts that will frame the answer, proposing a general argument and outlining the organisation of the essay are all ways of making sure that your essay is relevant to the set question and that the essay is an argument.

Activity 1.12 ....

Purpose: to look further at features of good essay introductions.

Task: Extracts 1.4 to 1.6 in Resource Book 2 are introductions to the same essay as in Activity 1.11. Using the table below each extract, repeat the process you carried out in Activity 1.11 and then decide whether any of the extracts might be considered **unsuccessful** introductions. Note down why you think this.

Compare your answers with those suggested in the Answer section.

Comment ....

A successful introduction provides a good foundation for an argument – but it is only the beginning.

Argument in essays – the body of the essay

There are many ways in which a good essay writer keeps control of the flow of the argument as they move through the text.

An essay text is a large unit of language made up of the following smaller units:

- text
- section
- paragraph
- sentence
- word group
- word.

To write a successful essay, each time you combine words into any of the larger units above, you have to control the flow of the argument.

To illustrate this, the next activity uses the essay introduced in Activity 1.11. The whole essay is in Resource Book 2, Text 1.7.

Activity 1.13 ....

Purpose: to see how a successful essay manages the flow of the argument from paragraph to paragraph.

Task: the answer to Activity 1.11 identifies three sets of words that are important to the argument of the essay:
- words which link back to the essay title
- words which identify key concepts in the essay
- words which state the central argument of the essay.

In Text 1.7 all these words are highlighted in the introduction. The key words are in *italic* type and the central argument is underlined.

Look at Text 1.7 in Resource Book 2. **You don't need to read it all.** Just read the first sentence in each paragraph, which is in **bold** type.

Using a highlighter or coloured pen, highlight any words in the first sentence of each paragraph which link back to the essay title, the key concepts in the introduction, or the central argument of the essay. The words you highlight don't have to be exactly the same as the ones in the introduction but they must be linked in some way.

Compare your answers with those suggested in the Answer section.

Comment ....

This essay manages the flow of the argument by using the first sentence of each paragraph to link back to the key concepts in the title and introduction, and the central statement of the argument. Each of these first sentences is a high-level **generalisation**. Each time the text moves up to one of these high levels, it links the reader back to the introduction and the paragraphs before, and the reader can see how the argument is developing.

As you will see in the next activity, these high-level generalisations are followed by lower levels of **details** and **examples** within the same paragraph. This movement up and down between high-level generalisations and lower-level details is the way the writer holds the argument together.

The links between the ideas in the argument are also reinforced by **linking or connecting words** in these first sentences, such as *another* aspect, *another* tool, *also* and *So in conclusion.*

It is important that the argument in an essay follows logically from the title.

Activity 1.14 ....

Purpose: to show that the flow of argument needs to follow logically from the title.

Task: Extract 1.8 in Resource Book 2 is a less successful essay with the same title as in Activity 1.11. It shows the introduction and the first sentence of each paragraph.

(a) Identify the key concepts and central argument in the introduction.

(b) Read the first sentence of each paragraph and decide how the writer controls the flow of the argument.

(c) Bearing in mind the three types of essay described earlier – description, explanation and discussion – which type do you think this student has written?

Compare your answers with those suggested in the Answer section.

Comment ....

A successful essay writer controls the flow of the argument *between* paragraphs and also the flow of the argument *within* each paragraph.

Argument in essays – paragraphs

In an explanation essay such as this, the flow of the argument within a paragraph can be controlled by:

1   Repeating concepts from previous sentences.

2   Moving up and down between high-level generalisations and lower-level details or examples.

3   Giving explanations by organising information into **cause–effect** sequences.

4   Using linking words which tie the sentences together.

5   Giving an **evaluation** of the ideas in previous sentences of the paragraph.

The next activity looks at how this is done in an example paragraph from Text 1.7.

Activity 1.15   ....

Purpose: to note how the flow of an argument is controlled in a paragraph.

Task 1: in Extract 1.9 the words at the beginning of each sentence are underlined. For each sentence decide whether these words:

(a) repeat a concept from the previous sentence (remember that they don't have to be exactly the same words to repeat a concept)

(b) are linking words which reinforce the connection between the sentences.

Task 2: is there any movement in the paragraph between high-level generalisations and lower-level details and examples?

Task 3: are any ideas joined together in a cause–effect sequence?

Task 4: are there any evaluations or judgements of the ideas from previous sentences?

Compare your answers with those suggested in the Answer section.

Comment   ....

This activity introduced some of the ways in which a writer makes the argument in an essay hold together. By using repetition, movement up and down between levels, cause–effect explanations, evaluations of ideas, and linking words, the writer builds a reasoned argument in the paragraph. The first sentences of the paragraphs hold each paragraph into the general argument of the essay; and they all link back to the introduction and the title.

This section introduced what tutors mean when they talk about 'argument'. In an explanation essay, the most important feature of an argument is that the reader can follow it clearly. In a discussion essay this is also important but it is also necessary to present more than one side to an argument. In a discussion essay, the question is not just 'Can you follow the argument?' It is also 'Do you agree with the argument?' The rest of this book will continue to explore how you can create arguments.

3 Use of source texts

If you use source material, your essay is based on other people's ideas. Some students have problems with this: either they find it difficult to convert the ideas they read into their own words or they prefer to present their own ideas instead of drawing on someone else's. However, tutors expect you to use other people's ideas. This is what studying a subject means. It is the key to a successful essay.

Here are some tutors' comments:

This is a thoughtfully argued essay based on wide reading and imaginative research.

What you say is all very well, but it is only one view. It happens to be the one I share but there is little evidence in this essay that you are aware of the objections which some writers have raised to it, or of some of the problems it raises.

(Clanchy and Ballard, 1998, p. 7)

Three skills are involved in using source materials.

1   Learning other people's ideas through reading and note making.

2   Turning these ideas into quotations, paraphrases or summaries.

3   Integrating the quotations, paraphrases and summaries into the essay. This includes linking them with the argument logically, making clear your own opinion about them and using a referencing method.

Extracts D and E below are examples of these skills being used in a student's essay.

Extract D	
Kotler et al. (1999, p. 5) even label Nike as the industry leader for development and it is interesting that this statement is not just limited to training shoes but all 'product development and innovation'.	**Source material turned into**: a summary and a short quotation. **Link with argument**: a judgement by a well-established expert is used to make a point. **Referencing method**: the author's name and the reporting verb, *label*, are used in the sentence; date and page number are in brackets. **Student's own opinion**: it is *interesting*.
Extract E	
Nike's 'Swoosh' logo is easily transferable and the brand message 'Just Do It' is appealing and acceptable to most cultures. This is expanded on by Bowman and Willis: 'Keeping the Nike Swoosh conservative and consistent allows it to become a unifying device across channels such as TV, print or Web, which tend to be anything but that' (2002, p. 87).	**Source material turned into**: long quotation. **Link with argument**: a well-established expert is used to add credibility to argument. **Referencing method**: source names and reporting verb, *expanded on*, in sentence; date and page number in brackets. **Student's own opinion**: not really given, but *expanded on* means this supports the idea previously given by the student.

Using source material is only successful if the material is integrated into the argument in your essay. In the next activity you begin to look at how source material was integrated into Text 1.7.

Activity 1.16   ....

Purpose: to explore some methods for integrating source material into an essay.

Task: look through Text 1.7 in Resource Book 2 and mark all the places where source material is referred to. Below are three descriptions of how source material is used in the text. Look at each of the examples you have marked in Text 1.7 and identify those of them which correspond to the descriptions below.

Description 1

Source material turned into: summary

Link with argument: statistical data from an expert

Referencing method: *according to* and author's name in sentence; date and page number in brackets

Student's own opinion: the sentence before and after the summary is supported by the data in the summary but there is no actual expression of student's opinion.

Description 2

Source material turned into: quotation

Link with argument: an opinion from an expert

Referencing method: all information is given in brackets

Student's own opinion: not given.

Description 3

Source material turned into: quotation

Link with argument: quotation supports the argument in the same sentence

Referencing method: author's name and the verb *explained* in the sentence; date and page number in brackets

Student's own opinion: not given.

Compare your answers with those suggested in the Answer section.

Comment ....

This activity has only begun to look at how source material is used in essays. These skills will be developed further in the rest of this course.

Source material is central to essay writing. Your tutor is unlikely to appreciate essays which don't use it. However, just including ideas from other sources is not enough. A tutor expects to see a critical and questioning attitude towards the source material. This critical attitude will be shown by what you choose to include, how you quote, paraphrase or summarise it, and the comments you make on it.

4 Appropriate presentation

Your tutor expects essays to be written in an academic style and that the grammar and spelling are reasonably accurate.

Here are some tutors' comments:

You tend to use words and ideas rather loosely, without being precise enough about what you mean.

Write in whole sentences, not stock phrases: take care with your spelling and your style of writing.

(Clanchy and Ballard, 1998, p. 10)

Academic style

You looked at the features of academic language style in Activities 1.2 and 1.4. You saw that, compared with spoken language, academic language tends to be more formal, more specialised, more abstract, more precise, and more careful about what is fact and what is opinion. As a result, successful academic writing is quite different from successful commercial writing or successful conversation.

Academic grammar

One of the main differences between spoken and written language is the way speakers and writers build up ideas. Speakers tend to add ideas together one after the other. Writers tend to pack ideas inside each other. This tight packing of ideas in academic writing calls for a particular kind of grammar which can be called *academic grammar*.

In each session of this book you will focus on different features of academic grammar. By the time you come to write an essay at the end of this book, you should have a good idea of which features you need to be careful about in your writing. In this session, you will look at the relationship between the **subject** and the **verb** of a sentence.

Agreement between subject and verb

> The business are succeeding.
>
>   Subject   Verb

In simple sentences such as the one above, it is fairly easy to see if the subject and the verb of the sentence do match – or **agree**, as this is termed grammatically.

Either the verb should be made **singular**: *is succeeding*

or the subject should be made **plural**: *businesses*.

This is the meaning of **subject–verb agreement**. However, it is sometimes less easy to follow the subject–verb agreement in academic sentences. Is there anything wrong with the next sentence?

> The 'just do it' slogan has had enormous success and the association of the product with prominent sport stars that have achieved great sporting results have encouraged sales.

The subject and the verb of the first clause in this sentence are both singular and are in agreement:

> The 'just do it' slogan has had enormous success ...
>
>   Subject   Verb

but the second subject is a very long noun group:

> the association of the product with prominent sport stars that have achieved great sporting results.

The main noun in this noun group is *the association* and it is a singular noun. But there is a plural noun in the group as well: *sport stars*.

When the writer eventually comes to the verb *have encouraged* they write the plural version. But, because the main noun in the noun group (*the association*) is singular, they should have written the singular verb, *has encouraged*.

Activity 1.17 ....

Purpose: to practise identifying the subject of a sentence when it is a long noun group and to edit sentences for subject–verb agreement.

Task 1: put brackets around the subjects of the following sentences and underline the main verb.

Task 2: check that the subject–verb agreement is correct.

1   The focus on research and development and distribution rather than actual manufacture, while no longer offering a unique advantage over competitors, still allow Nike to lead the field.

2   Focusing on developing its brand and relying on other organisations to manufacture its product has meant Nike can concentrate on its marketing and distribution.

3   It is also necessary to describe how Nike's approach to some of the key business areas such as marketing, design and technology, manufacturing and distribution have contributed to their success.

4   Phil Knight has developed a unique working environment for his employees that allow them to perform and succeed at a high standard.

5   A product range that delivers high sports performance – designing for Pete Sampras and Andre Agassi – while offering a distinct and appealing appearance and image that has become a fashion accessory of this decade are integrated into modern cultures such as Brit pop and hip-hop music scene.

Compare your answers with those suggested in the Answer section.

Comment ....

Sometimes the reason for incorrect subject–verb agreement is that the writer has tried to pack too much information into a sentence. However, it is difficult to write academically without packing in information, so it is a good idea to check the subject–verb agreement for any long subject nouns.

Academic vocabulary

In academic writing, specialised academic words are important. However, using specialised vocabulary is more than just using individual words such as *marketing* or *manufacturing*. It also means knowing how to use words in specialised combinations, such as *marketing strategy* or *outsourcing manufacturing*. For this reason it is important to learn the words that combine with other specialised business words.

The next activity introduces specialised word combinations.

Activity 1.18

Purpose: to introduce the idea of word combinations.

Task 1: the two lists of words below are from Text 1.7. In that essay they are used in word combinations. These combinations are mixed up below. Find each word in the left-hand column in the essay and match it with the word that it combines with in the right-hand column. Then do Task 2.

success	appeal
marketing	campaign
company	mission
leading	strategy
advertising	approach
advertising	brand
labour	intensive
outsource	manufacture
company	responsibility
corporate	story
consumer	success
commercial	markets
innovative	priority
target	slogan

Task 2: insert a suitable word combination from Text 1.7 in the sentences below which are from other essays on Nike.

(a) One of the key factors that have contributed to the Nike _____ is how the company markets, designs and sells its product.

(b) A successful _____ is key to giving the brand a high profile, as 'sales are in effect determined by the way in which training shoes are marketed to the consumer' (Sturges, 2000, p. 32).

(c) 'Just do it', which is 'now acknowledged to be one of the best-known _____ of the twentieth century' (Sturges, 2000, p. 33), is said to have inspired people to make radical decisions.

(d) The process itself is very _____ due to the large number of individual parts involved and the relatively handmade nature of trainers.

(e) For Nike it still makes financial sense to _____ to these companies rather than setting up its own production plants in America with its higher wages, shorter hours and trade unions.

Compare your answers with those suggested in the Answer section.

Comment

Academic language and business language are full of specialised words. Both kinds of language are sometimes criticised for using words only to create a clever impression. However, in business studies you cannot avoid this language. You need to decide which words are important because they will help you communicate more effectively and which ones are just being used to make an impression.

1.4 Critical reflection

Just like an essay, this session presented an argument. It put forward a point of view about what university essays are like and what university tutors expect. As suggested earlier, there are two questions to ask about an argument: 'Can you follow it?' and 'Do you agree with it?' You will consider these questions in this section on critical reflection.

Activity 1.19

Purpose: to check your understanding of the argument in this session.

Task: write a short summary of the argument in this session.

There is no answer to this activity.

1.5 A whole essay

Activity 1.20   ....

Purpose: to apply the ideas from this session to a whole essay.

Task: Text 1.10 in Resource Book 2 is the essay you read in the previous activities. Down the right-hand side there are notes which describe how the ideas in the essay are linked to make an argument. In 10 places, the notes are missing and there is a gap. The missing notes are in the mixed-up list below. Read each paragraph of the essay and then read the notes. For each gap, find the missing note from the list below.

(a) Quotation is given as evidence for the idea that *innovation* is important.

(b) The paragraph reviews several concepts from the body of the essay.

(c) Links to the key concept of *success* from paragraph 1 (*Philip Knight's business skills*).

(d) Introduces two key concepts that frame the essay (*marketing and innovation*).

(e) New concept word (*exclusivity*) frames this paragraph.

(f) Gives details to explain the concept *innovation*.

(g) Gives argument against *outsourcing*.

(h) Range of concepts are linked to *marketing strategy* and gives examples.

(i) Repeats the theme of *success* from the introduction.

(j) In first sentence the key concept *advertising* links back to previous paragraph and frames this paragraph.

Compare your answers with those suggested in the Answer section.

1.6 Review

In this session you:

- compared the purpose, organisation, language and reader–writer relationship of an essay text with a company website presentation and an online discussion

- were introduced to the four characteristics that tutors look for when they read an essay: relevance, argument, source material and presentation

- considered what 'argument' means in an essay, and

- looked at some differences between writing an essay and speaking.

1.7 Answer section

Activity 1.1

Extract 1.1 – company website; Extract 1.2 – sports shoe discussion website; Extract 1.3 – business studies essay.

Activity 1.2

Informal   Formal

SS		CW		E

The language features which make the sports shoe extract (SS) informal also make it seem more personal and more spoken than written, including:

1   The language of casual conversation: *I'm almost lost for the right words.*

2   Language that directly addresses the reader: *I think after playing many minutes in these, you'll pick up on the weight factor.*

3   Language about the personal experience of the writer: *probably the most comfortable Bball shoes in my collection of hoop shoes.*

4   Short sentences or sentences made up of several short parts added together.

5   Language belonging to a specialised 'in-group', which may not be known to people outside that group: *hoop shoes.*

The language of the Nike website (CW) has some of the same informal language features (for example, *the guy was right*), although it also has a more written style, the sentences have a more organised structure, and there are some technical terms which increase the formality: *focused on creating performance opportunities for everyone who would benefit.*

The student's essay (E) is generally very formal. The writer is detached from the subject and does not write about their experience. There is no direct reference to the reader. The words chosen are specialised business studies words. These belong to a different kind of 'in-group' – an academic one. This uses a formal style of language compared with that of the sports shoe review. The sentences are longer and seem carefully organised.

Personal   Impersonal

SS	CW			E

Everyday style/non-specialist   Technical/specialist

	CW		SS	E

Easy to read   Difficult to read

CW?		SS?	E?		

Your answer to the scale above depends partly on your previous reading experience. All three texts are written to be easy to read, but they are written for different readers, so it depends what kind of reader you are.

Loosely organised text   Strongly organised text

SS				CW, E

As these are extracts, you cannot see how the whole texts are organised. However, the sentences in the sports shoe review are less carefully organised than in the other two extracts. It is as if the sentences have been put in the order that they came into the writer's mind. The other two texts look as if they have been planned more carefully. You will examine this further in Activity 1.4.

More speech-like   More writing-like

SS		CW		E

Some of the features that make a text informal are also the features that make it more speech-like. The difference between spoken and written language is explained in more detail in Activity 1.4.

Activity 1.3

Extract 1.1	*Extract 1.2*	*Extract 1.3*
Why was the text written?		
✓ to create a good impression of Nike	✓ to review a new training shoe design	✓ to learn about company performance in the modern business world ✓ to explain why Nike is the largest sports and fitness company in the world
Who is the writer?		
✓ a public relations officer	✓ an athlete ✓ a public relations officer	✓a student
Who is the reader?		
✓ the general public ✓ athletes	✓ the general public ✓ athletes	✓ a tutor

Activity 1.4

Some examples are given below; you might have chosen different examples.

More spoken style	More written style
Context-dependent	**Context-independent**
Extract 1.1 *we remain; ours is a language*	Extract 1.1 *Bill Bowerman said this* (the words are not being spoken now)
Extract 1.2 *these are, this shoe, in these*	Extract 1.2 All very context-dependent
Extract 1.3 None	Extract 1.3 *The use of the famous 'Just do it' advertising slogan* (rather than this slogan)
Personal	**Impersonal**
Extract 1.1 *Ours is a language; we*	Extract 1.1 *for everyone who would benefit* (not for you)
Extract 1.2 *in my collection; I'm so pleased*	Extract 1.2 None
Extract 1.3 None	Extract 1.3 *The technique of communicating is paramount* (not they communicate very well)
Informal, colloquial, everyday language	**Formal, specialised language**
Extract 1.1 *the guy; downright embarrassing*	Extract 1.1 *creating performance opportunities*
Extract 1.2 *traction is top-notch*	Extract 1.2 *did a walk through; hoop shoes*
Extract 1.3 There is some colloquial language in the sentence about the famous *'Just do it' slogan* but this is because it is reporting on the Nike style, which is informal	Extract 1.3 *marketing strategy, image, symbolic status of goods, emotional appeal*
Many, generally short, clauses joined by simple conjunctions	**Long noun groups, longer clauses, more complicated conjunctions**
Extract 1.1 *The guy was right*	Extract 1.1 *We remain totally focused ... etc.*
Extract 1.2 *I did drills for a bit and tried ...*	Extract 1.2 None
Extract 1.3 None	Extract 1.3 *The use of the famous 'Just do it' advertising slogan ... etc.*

Activity 1.5

(1) define; (2) compare and contrast; (3) explain; (4) discuss.

Activity 1.6

List 1

Analyse	(b) take apart an idea, concept or statement in order to consider all the factors it consists of. It should be very methodically and logically organised.
Compare	(a) look for similarities **and** differences between the items under discussion.
Contrast	(d) look for differences between the items ideas under discussion
Summarise	(c) write about the main points of the information available on a subject and not the details.

List 2

Define	(c) state precisely what is meant by a particular issue, theory or concept.
Describe	(d) give a detailed account of.
Discuss	(b) give reasons for and against; investigate and examine by argument.
Evaluate	(a) weigh up the arguments surrounding an issue, using your own opinions and, more importantly, reference to the work of others.

List 3

Assess	(c) make comments about the value/importance of the concepts and ideas under discussion.
Illustrate	(a) make clear by the use of example.
Explain	(b) make something clear or give reasons for something.

Activity 1.7

1. From your understanding **of the organisational context for management**, define the terms '**environment**' and '**structure**'.
2. Compare and contrast hard **Human Resource Management approaches** with **soft ones**.
3. Explain **Porter's concept of the Value Chain** and comment on its **implications** for **the design of organisations**.
4. Explain why **Nike** is **the biggest training shoe company in the world**.
5. Discuss how **business processes** might affect **an organisation's ability to compete effectively**.

Activity 1.8

Linked key concepts: Value Chain – design of organisations.

Words indicating the link: <u>its implications</u> for the design of organisations.

Activity 1.9

1. <u>From your understanding</u> of the organisational context for management, define the terms 'environment' and 'structure'.
2. <u>Compare and contrast</u> hard Human Resource Management approaches with soft ones.
3. Explain Porter's concept of the Value Chain and <u>comment on its implications</u> for the design of organisations.
4. Explain <u>why</u> Nike is the biggest training shoe company in the world.
5. Discuss <u>how</u> business processes <u>might affect</u> an organisation's ability to compete effectively.

Activity 1.10

2   How do hard Human Resource Management approaches compare with soft ones?

3   What is Porter's concept of the Value Chain? How does it work? What are its implications for the design of organisations?

4   Why is Nike the biggest training shoe company in the world?

5   How might business processes affect an organisation's ability to compete effectively?

Activity 1.11

Words which link back to the title	*biggest = successful, leading brand*
Words which identify the key concepts in the essay	*success* *two strategies: marketing and innovation*
Words which state the central argument of the essay	*This essay will examine how the marketing strategy and the company mission ... have made the company into a leading brand throughout the world.*
Words which say how the essay will be organised	There are no specific words about the essay organisation although the sentence which states the central argument gives a good idea about the organisation of the essay.

Activity 1.12

Extract 1.4

Words which link back to the title	*Nike* but there is no clear link to the idea that Nike is the biggest training shoe company.
Words which identify the key concepts in the essay	It is difficult to be sure. *Trainers* is the only word which is definitely key.
Words which state the central argument of the essay	There are several general statements in this introduction. Any of them could become the argument of the essay – or none.
Words which say how the essay will be organised	The essay is not referred to at all.

Extract 1.5

Words which link back to the title	*Nike*: there is a reference to *increase Nike's image* but no other obvious links.
Words which identify the key concepts in the essay	The key concepts seem to be *outsourcing*, *quality control*, *corporate responsibility* and *Nike image*. However, there is no obvious link between these and the title or the argument of the essay.
Words which state the central argument of the essay	None: any of the ideas here could become the argument.
Words which say how the essay will be organised	None

Extract 1.6

Words which link back to the title	*biggest training shoe company in the world; clearly dominating; achieved this position because of; Nike's combined success ... into a market leader.*
Words which identify the key concepts in the essay	*timely recognition of the nature of the market; innovative philosophy and management style; inspired marketing campaign.*
Words which state the central argument of the essay	*I will argue ... because of three factors.*
Words which say how the essay will be organised	*I will argue ... because of three factors.*

Extracts 1.4 and 1.5 are not successful introductions.

Activity 1.13

Nike was launched in the USA in 1972 by Philip Knight, a former university runner with **strong business acumen** and his university coach, Bill Bowerman.

For Nike to compete with other brands of training shoe it has developed a **marketing strategy** to make the Nike brand highly desirable.

Training shoe companies invest a great deal of money in **advertising to promote their products** and convey the concept of emotional appeal.

Another aspect of the Nike **marketing strategy** is to use the technique of exclusivity to **bolster the appeal of the brand.**

Innovation is another tool in the Nike success story, innovation in both business and technological terms.

Nike has also been innovative in its design and technology application.

So in conclusion, **the innovative approach of Nike** of reducing overheads by outsourcing manufacturing of the training shoes in countries where labour costs are low, combined with **focus on design and marketing** has secured **Nike the position of biggest training shoe company in the world.**

Activity 1.14

(a) and (b): the main argument in the essay seems to be about *how Nike developed.* This is not really what the title asks for, which is *why* Nike became the biggest training shoe company in the world.

(c) This is really a description essay. The ideas are linked together by time linking words rather than by argument as follows.

Nike is a brand that a large majority of people are familiar with, but many know less about **the history of the company** and **the impact it has on society.** This paper will investigate how Nike developed. The company has grown very rapidly from a small business idea in the University of Oregon. In 1966 Nike opened its first retail outlet in a narrow building at 3107 Pico Blvd in Santa Monica. In the first year they made just $364 and by 1969 sales had risen to a million dollars. Since then it has developed every year.

Since 1995 Nike has **tripled its design** budget and employs over 300 designers.

In 1998 Nike spent £10 million on advertising trainers in the UK alone.

It is reported that the Nike sponsorship deal with golfer Tiger Woods is worth $90 million.

By 2004, Nike had **43% market share** in the US.

Close to 1 million people work for Nike.

So, there can be no doubt that **Nike is the biggest training shoe company** in the world.

Activity 1.15

Some of the possible links in the argument flow are as follows.

Task 1: (a) The production of a training shoe; factories; the company; a potentially bad situation. (b) As mentioned previously; This strategy; But.

Task 2: business innovation – outsource manufacture to South East Asia.

Task 3: the ideas are joined by *so*, *saves*, *thus*.

Task 4: a potentially bad situation.

Activity 1.16

1   ... Tom Vanderbilt (1998, p. 66) explained, '... design is what makes the product exciting ...'
2   According to Sturges, in 1998 Nike spent £10 million ...
3   Nike's advertising campaigns seek to 'shift the selling point away from the product itself and into a world of their own making' (Vanderbilt, 1998).

Activity 1.17

1   [The focus on research and development and distribution rather than actual manufacture,] <u>allow</u> (should be *allows*).
2   [Focusing on developing its brand and relying on other organisations to manufacture its product] <u>has meant</u> (should be *have meant*).
3   It is also necessary to describe how [Nike's approach to some of the key business areas such as marketing, design and technology, manufacturing and distribution] <u>have contributed</u> (should be *has contributed*).
4   Phil Knight has developed [a unique working environment for his employees that] <u>allow</u> (should be *allows*).

5   [A product range that delivers high sports performance – designing for Pete Sampras and Andre Agassi – while offering a distinct and appealing appearance and image that has become a fashion accessory of this decade] <u>are integrated</u> (should be *is integrated*).

Activity 1.18

Task 1

success	story
marketing	strategy
company	mission
leading	brand
advertising	slogan
advertising	campaign
labour	intensive
outsource	manufacture
company	priority
corporate	responsibility
consumer	appeal
commercial	success
innovative	approach
target	markets

Task 2

(a) success story; (b) marketing strategy; (c) advertising slogans; (d) labour intensive; (e) outsource manufacture.

Activity 1.20

1   Introduces two key concepts that frame essay (*marketing and innovation*).
2   Links to key concept of success from paragraph 1 (*Philip Knight's business skills*).
3   Range of concepts are linked to marketing strategy and give examples.
4   In first sentence the key concept advertising links back to previous paragraph and frames this paragraph.
5   New concept word (*exclusivity*) frames this paragraph.
6   Gives details to explain the concept *innovation*.
7   Gives argument against outsourcing.
8   Quotation is given as evidence for the idea that innovation is important.
9   Repeats the theme of success from introduction.
10   The paragraph reviews several concepts from the body of the essay.

SESSION **2 The process of essay writing**

2.1 Introduction

In answering the question 'What is an essay?', Session 1 highlighted the distinctiveness of essays compared with other forms of writing. In this session you will focus on **how** to write essays.

This course has regularly referred to the concept of a systems model consisting of inputs and outputs. What you do to the inputs to convert them to outputs is a form of processing. Book 1 outlined the processes involved in converting inputs into a **case study analysis**. This book examines the processes involved in producing an **essay.**

It is much easier to understand the processes involved in producing something if you know what the goal or the end product is. Session 1 introduced the various features of an essay, giving you a clearer idea of what you should aim to produce.

This session examines the processes box in the middle of the essay-production diagram, while Session 3 looks at the outputs box, that is, essay design.

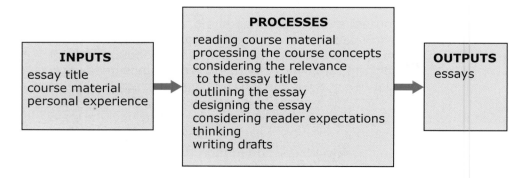

Figure 2.1   Producing an essay

Learning outcomes

In this session you will:

- analyse an essay title to be clear about its requirements
- brainstorm ideas for an essay
- use an essay-writing checklist
- learn how to select and manage essay source materials
- apply active reading techniques to a selection of source materials
- practise note-making skills
- plan an essay
- write an essay outline.

This session focuses on two essay titles. The first title is used to **model** the skills and processes involved in essay writing while the second title is the one you will **practise** these skills and processes on in preparation for producing a draft essay to send to your tutor.

2.2   Step 1: Analysing the essay title

Focusing on the instructions

The first step in writing an essay is to be clear about what you are being asked to do.

As explained in Session 1, an essay title may contain some or all of the following components:

- an introductory statement about the topic
- instruction words
- key concepts
- guidelines about the scope of the essay.

You will begin by comparing two essay titles.

Activity 2.1 ....

Purpose: to identify the components of two essay titles.

Task: look at the two essay titles below. Which of the above components does each one contain?

(A) Explain why Nike is the biggest training shoe company in the world.

(B) Discuss the extent to which a large corporation such as Nike might influence the economic health of a developing country.

Compare your answers with those suggested in the Answer section.

Comment ....

Both essay titles contain an instruction word. As indicated in Session 1, *explain* and *discuss* may be distinguished by the fact that 'discuss' requires you to incorporate your opinion of the topic in question.

Both titles include several key concepts, which are explored in more detail below.

They both also contain a reference to **scope**. Essay title A refers specifically and exclusively to Nike, while essay title B uses the phrase *a large corporation such as Nike*. In essay title A the focus is on a single company – Nike. In essay title B the scope is broader, the focus being on *large corporations* in general, with Nike as a possible example. You may refer to the practices of similar businesses if you have such information.

Focusing on key concepts

You have already worked with key concepts many times in this course. The key concepts of an essay title are the foundations on which the piece of writing should be built. They provide the basis for the **framing** of your essay. As such they should direct your pre-reading activities, the identification of appropriate sources of input material, the notes that you take and the planning and organisation of your essay. Therefore, it is important that you understand exactly what these key concepts mean and what they include or exclude.

First, identify the key concepts in essay title A which you examined above:

> Explain why Nike is the biggest training shoe company in the world.

Its key concepts are *Nike* and *biggest training shoe company in the world*.

Now you will do the same for essay title B.

Activity 2.2 ....

Purpose: to identify the key concepts in an essay title.

Task: underline the key concepts in essay title B:

'Discuss the extent to which a large corporation such as Nike might influence the economic health of a developing country.'

Compare your answers with those suggested in the Answer section.

Comment ....

As explained in Session 1, it is important not only to identify the key concepts in an essay title but also to recognise how they are **linked**. This link often forms the basis of the essay. What is the connection between the key concepts in essay title B?

The important word here is *influence*. This is one of the **cause–effect** words that you encountered in Book 1. In this essay title, the activity of large corporations is the **cause** and the economic health of the developing countries in which they work is the **effect**.

The next three activities are intended to help you question your understanding of the concepts which you identified in essay title B. In working through each activity, it is not important that you get the 'correct' answers (in some cases, there aren't any). What matters is that you take the time to reflect on these key concepts, while noting any gaps in your understanding. You will then be more attentive to this information when reading the source materials in preparation for the draft essay that you will write at the end of this session.

Activity 2.3 ....

Purpose: to consider your understanding of the key concepts of essay title B in more detail.

Task 1: name any other large corporations – or multinational companies (MNCs) – that might be considered similar to Nike. List them below. An example is provided to get you started.

Coca-Cola

_____

_____

_____

Task 2: what factors do you think indicate that a country is in good economic health?

Choose from the words in the left-hand column below and combine them with the words in the right-hand column. Note: some words may be used more than once.

rising	
falling	prices
high	inflation
low	employment
stable	living standards
fluctuating	balance of payments
a healthy	

Task 3

(a) list some examples of **developing countries** below.

_____

_____

_____

_____

(b) How would you define a developing country? Think of the features that differentiate it from a developed country. Write down your definition in the space below.

_____

_____

_____

(c) Various terms are used to refer to 'developing' and 'developed' countries. Some of them are listed below. Sort them into two columns, one headed 'Developing countries' and the other headed 'Developed countries'. Add any other expressions that you have met. Which term(s) do you prefer? Why?

underdeveloped countries	industrialised nations	undeveloped countries
the Third World	the West	the First World
the Majority World	the South	LEDCs
western countries	MEDCs	non-industrialised nations

Compare your answers with those suggested in the Answer section.

Rewording the title

Sometimes students think they have understood the instructions in an essay title, yet then don't follow them correctly. This can result in a considerable loss of marks. Therefore, it is always worth double-checking your understanding of the instructions. One way of doing this is to consider what alternative wording might mean the same as the given title.

Activity 2.4   ....

Purpose: to examine an essay title more closely by considering which alternative titles are equivalent to its meaning.

Task: which of the alternative titles below mean the same as essay title A? Mark them with tick (✓) or a cross (✗).

Compare your answers with those suggested in the Answer section.

A Explain why Nike is the biggest training shoe company in the world.	✓ ✗
1 Why is Nike the biggest training shoe company in the world?	
2 Is Nike the biggest training shoe company in the world?	
3 How has Nike become the biggest training shoe company in the world?	
4 In what ways is Nike the biggest training shoe company in the world?	
5 What are the reasons behind Nike's success?	

Comment ....

Note how all of the alternative titles are questions. This is because – even if the original essay title is not in the form of a question (that is, it does not start with a word such as 'why' or 'how' and does not end with a question mark) – it usually has a question at its heart. An early step in the essay-writing process is to identify this underlying question as it will provide a clear focus for you in preparing your response. Note that there may be slight variations in the wording of the underlying question, as demonstrated by the possible answers to this activity.

Fact and opinion-oriented essay titles

An important distinction between essay titles A and B concerns the difference between the notions of **fact** and **opinion**.

Look at both essay titles again.

(A) Explain why Nike is the biggest training shoe company in the world.

(B) Discuss the extent to which a large corporation such as Nike might influence the economic health of a developing country.

Note how in essay title A the idea that 'Nike is the biggest training shoe company in the world' is presented as an established fact. The essay title does not ask whether you agree that this is the case or not. Rather it assumes – perhaps on the basis of the input and associated readings available – that this is shared knowledge. Your task is to focus on the causes leading to this state of affairs.

Now consider essay title B. In what ways does it differ from essay title A?

Activity 2.5 ....

Purpose: to note the difference between fact and opinion-oriented essay titles.

Task: underline any words or expressions in essay title B that suggest it is not a fact-oriented essay like essay title A.

Compare your answer with that suggested in the Answer section.

Comment ....

Essay title B is different from essay title A in that it does not assume an established, shared acceptance of a particular state of affairs. Rather it asks for your **opinion** on the topic in question.

By using the word *might* before the phrase *influence the economic health of a developing country*, the essay title suggests that it is possible to disagree with the idea that large corporations influence the economic health of developing countries.

Might is an example of a **modal verb**. You first encountered these in Book 1 where they were used to propose solutions. Here they are being used to express **opinion**. Other modals which can express opinion are *may*, *could* and *should*.

The expression *the extent* is used to request your judgement on **how much** influence large corporations have on the economic health of a developing country.

The essay therefore requires you to give your **views** on the **causal relationship** between the activity of large corporations and the economic health of developing countries, specifically:

- **How much** and **in what ways** do large corporations influence the economic health of developing countries?
- Is this influence **positive**, **negative** or a **mixture** of both?

Of course, it would be possible to put forward a case **against** fact-oriented titles such as essay title A. However, it could be argued that this does not really amount to answering the question! More seriously, challenging conventional wisdom in this way tends to be the domain of writers with extensive knowledge of an area, who are more practised in accessing and interpreting the evidence available.

2.3 Step 2: Pre-reading activities

While it may be tempting to start reading for your essay as quickly as you can, you will find that a little preparation for this will make your reading much more efficient.

A good starting point is to establish what you know and don't know about the topic to be written about. In exploring your understanding of the key concepts of the essay title in Activity 2.2, you have already begun this process.

Brainstorming

The next step is to use the key concepts as the basis for a brainstorming activity in which you note down all that you can associate with a particular topic area. You may remember this technique from Book 1, where you also learned about mind mapping as a means of organising information in a visual way.

When applied to the key concepts of an essay title, brainstorming mind maps can help you draw out and group the knowledge and ideas that you have about these topics, while at the same time highlighting any gaps that need to be followed up in your reading.

Book 1 also introduced the recommended academic technique of **questioning**. The key concepts in an essay title should not be used simply as prompts for noting down associated knowledge and ideas but for asking questions. Questioning can refine your understanding of the essay title and help you engage further with the topic.

What questions might you want to ask about the key concepts in essay title A, 'Explain why Nike is the biggest training shoe company in the world'?

One possible question to ask is: What does 'biggest' mean in this context?

What answers might there be to this question? It can be helpful to note down some ideas even if you are guessing or unsure at this stage.

Figure 2.2 is a mind map of a student's initial brainstorming for essay title A, using the key concepts as initial prompts. You will see that already there is an attempt at grouping the subject matter into sub-topics. By asking questions, the student is probing the key concepts further. Note too how she uses question marks alongside the ideas that she is not entirely sure are relevant at this stage.

Is this similar to how you would have done a brainstorming mind map for this essay title? Is there anything else you might have added?

Now it is your turn to create a pre-reading brainstorming mind map.

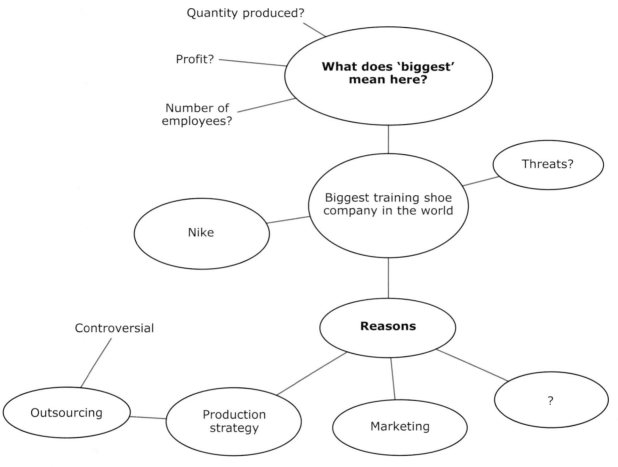

Figure 2.2 Student's initial mind map of essay title A

Activity 2.6 ....

Purpose: to practise doing a brainstorming mind map on an essay title.

Task: now create your own brainstorming mind map based on essay title B. Focus in particular on any questions that you have about:
- the key concepts that you have identified for this essay
- other aspects of the essay title, such as its opinion-oriented slant (Activity 2.5).

You will need to refer back and add to this mind map later in this session, so keep it to hand.

There is no suggested answer for this activity because this task is concerned with generating your own ideas.

2.4 Step 3: Reading for essay writing

Once you have established the exact requirements of the essay title, identified its key concepts and used these as the basis for creating a brainstorming mind map, you will have a better idea of the big picture within which the task is situated. You will also be more aware of the limitations of your knowledge about aspects of the topic.

The next step is to consider what can help you understand the subject under consideration. In the case of a business essay, this input will probably consist of reading material such as chapters of books, articles in journals or newspapers, web-based texts, and – where appropriate – case studies.

Reading is not only a means of finding **information** that is relevant to the essay requirements. It will also help you build up the **language** associated with the subject area being explored.

Reading techniques

Book 1, Session 1 introduced an active reading method which involved several different techniques. You have had many opportunities to practise using them when studying this course book and its associated Resource Book.

Activity 2.7 ....

Purpose: to review the active reading method that you met in Book 1.

Task 1: in the space below, list as many of the techniques that you can remember from the active reading method described in Book 1.

_____

_____

_____

_____

_____

_____

When you have finished, group these techniques according to whether they are:

(a) pre-reading activities

(b) during-reading activities

(c) post-reading activities.

Compare your answers with those suggested in the Answer section.

Task 2: now consider the following questions.

How useful do you find this reading method?

Do some of these techniques work for you better than others? Mark those that you regularly use in your course reading with a tick.

Do you always follow the techniques in the same order?

Have you added any further techniques of your own?

Selecting appropriate source materials

A checklist for a successful essay

Session 1 introduced the four characteristics of a successful essay: relevance to the essay title, a reasoned argument, good use of source materials, and appropriate presentation.

In business studies courses, tutors usually have a clear idea about which business concepts and ideas they expect you to be working with in an essay. They are very likely to have a checklist of them, which they will use to assess you.

In courses on professional communication skills such as this one, tutors are looking at not only **what** ideas are included in an essay but also **how** they are communicated. They will use a checklist to assess these features too.

This session introduces a checklist of criteria for successful communication in essays. The whole checklist is reproduced in the Appendix for your information. This checklist will be used to assess your communication skills in the assignment that you will write on completing this book.

Being familiar with the different elements that contribute to a good essay will give you a better understanding of what is expected with this kind of writing. It will also help with editing your work and reviewing the work of other people. These skills are the focus of Session 6.

In this session the focus is on the first set of criteria of the checklist: **use of source material** (Box 2.1). Don't be concerned if initially you don't understand some of the terminology. It will gradually become clearer to you. The other sets of criteria are considered in subsequent sessions of this book.

Box 2.1   Checklist for a successful essay

A   *Use of source material – is information from study and research correct and appropriate for the task?*

1   Relevant information from reading is used
2   Irrelevant information from reading is avoided
3   Information from reading or other research is interpreted correctly
4   Information from reading or other research is transferred correctly
5   Information is integrated with the text
6   Text is free from plagiarism
7   Bibliography is constructed correctly

Source: adapted from materials created by Helen Bonano and Janet Jones, MASUS Project, University of Sydney, 1997.

As mentioned above, this checklist outlines the key features of a successful essay. Therefore, it focuses on the final **product** in Figure 2.1. This session is concerned with the **processes** involved in achieving a successful essay or end product. The following activities will together contribute to this overall goal.

Locating source materials

Some people imagine that a single text exists which will contain everything they need to know, ideally presented in the required order, to respond to the essay title. This is most unlikely.

At times you will be provided with recommended reading in connection with a particular essay or task. At other times you may need to supplement this list with other sources of information or identify all the reading material yourself. Whatever is the case, you will need to read a range of materials, interpret their content, combine selected ideas with your own, and organise them into a coherent argument.

Being selective

Whether searching for paper-based or internet resources, it is important to learn to discriminate between the different texts that may contain information about the topic that you are interested in.

How should you choose from the many sources of information available to you? A key factor in such a choice is its **relevance**. A source text is relevant if it is appropriate, trustworthy and reliable with respect to a particular **purpose**.

Activity 2.8 ....

Purpose: to consider the relevance of a selection of texts to a particular purpose.

Task: read through the texts listed in Table 2.2 and tick those which are more likely to be **relevant** sources of input for essay title B, which you are working towards:

Discuss the extent to which a large corporation such as Nike might influence the economic health of a developing country.

Compare your answers with those suggested in the Answer section.

Table 2.2

No.	Text reference	Type of text	Relevant?
1	www.nike.com/nikebiz/nikebiz.jhtml?page=3	Nike's official company website	
2	Sturges, J. (2000) 'Keep on running: the training shoe business' The Open University Business School, Milton Keynes.	Case study on Nike	
3	Vanderbilt, T. (1998) *The Sneaker Book: Anatomy of an Industry and an Icon*, The New Press, New York, NY.	Book which explores the significance and global impact of the training shoe industry.	
4	The official LBJ IV review Post!!! http://shoes.about.com/gi/dynamic/offsite.htm?zi=1/XJ/Ya&sdn=shoes&cdn=style&tm=60&gps=168_815_962_555&f=00&tt=14&bt=1&bts=1&zu =http%3A//niketalk.com/	Training shoe discussion website (see Session 1)	
5	http://en.wikipedia.org/wiki/Nike,_Inc.	General information on Nike	
6	http://news.bbc.co.uk/hi/english/static/audio_video/programmes/panorama/transcripts/transcript_15_10_00.txt	Transcript of BBC documentary: *Gap and Nike: No Sweat?*, 15 October 2000	
7	Sloman, J. and Sutcliffe, M. (1998) 'When markets fail' in Suneja, M. (ed.) *Understanding Business: Markets*, Routledge, London, pp. 117–144	Chapter on multinational companies in developing countries. In OU business course materials	
8	www.oxfam.org.au/campaigns/labour/index.html	'Just stop it!', Oxfam Australia's campaign to persuade sports brands to respect workers' rights	
9	www.gso.gov.vn/ default_en.aspx?tabid=476&idmid=4&ItemID=1841	Government of Vietnam Population and Housing Census, Vietnam, 1999	
10	www.britannica.com/eb/question-628349/18/GNP-Vietnam	*Encyclopaedia Britannica* online: GNP of Vietnam	

Comment ....

One of the factors to consider when assessing the *relevance* of a particular source text for a business essay is whether the author or publisher is reliable and trustworthy.

Universities, government agencies and established charities are likely sources of reliable information (note that their web addresses often incorporate the abbreviation 'ac', 'gov' or 'org'), as are company-produced documents, such as reports and accounts.

Wikipedia and *The Encyclopaedia Britannica* – while providing useful information – are not normally accepted as appropriate for university study because their content is not developed for university purposes.

An important consideration when assessing the relevance of particular source materials is what **bias**, if any, a particular text might have. Nike's company website may be a good authority for statistics about company performance, for example, but it would probably be considered a less appropriate source of objective information on the company's influence on developing countries. What is important is that you are aware that sources may contain a particular bias. You should therefore approach them with that in mind. That is the essence of critical reading. This skill is covered in more detail in Session 4.

The date of publication may also be a factor in deciding whether one source of information is more relevant than another. More recent publications tend to contain more up-to-date information, but it is important to be cautious here as this is not always the case.

Your tutor can guide you if you are not sure which additional sources to use in your essay writing.

Primary and secondary sources

A distinction to be aware of in academic reading is that between primary sources on the one hand and secondary sources on the other.

Primary sources are **real world** data. They include any original documents, such as figures, diaries, recordings of interviews and responses to questionnaires. Secondary sources are **one step away** from primary sources in that they **compile**, **interpret** and **comment on** those original documents or data.

An example of a primary source would be the transcripts of interviews with workers in a Nike factory in China conducted by an international charity concerned with workers' rights. A secondary source would be a report which includes an analysis of those interviews.

The primary source – the real world data – can be considered **evidence**, while the secondary source provides an **explanation** – or a means of interpreting – the data. These two notions – evidence and explanation – are examined more closely in Session 3.

A case study is an interesting example as it is a mixture of primary and secondary material designed to represent the real world. However, it is normally viewed as a primary source of information.

Whether you are looking at primary or secondary sources – that is, real world data or a commentary on it – what matters is that they are both relevant and reliable with respect to the requirements of your essay.

Recommended source materials

Essay title B is accompanied by guidance notes which recommend reading the following input texts.

- Sturges, J. (2000) 'Keep on running: the training shoe business', The Open University Business School, Milton Keynes (Text 2.1). This is extracts from a case study about Nike.

- Lucas, M. (2000) *Environments. Module 1 Study Guide*, The Open University Business School, Milton Keynes, pp. 22–30 (Text 2.2). This is an adapted chapter of an Open University business course which explores several of the business concepts that are relevant to this essay title. It also acts as an introduction to the extracts from the chapter by Coates below.

- Coates, D. (2000) 'The management of the UK economy', in Lucas M. (ed.) *Understanding Business: Environments*, Routledge, London, pp. 55–70 (Text 2.3). These extracts are part of a more theoretical article about how economies work.

Bearing in mind the distinction made above, which of these three texts might provide **evidence**? Which might provide an **explanation**?

Text 2.1 may be considered the **evidence** or real world data. Texts 2.2 and 2.3, in contrast, provide an **explanation** or a theoretical framework for viewing and interpreting the data.

In the following activities you will read and make notes on each text in turn. The outputs will together contribute to the task at the end of this session – the production of a draft essay for essay title B. You will send this draft to your tutor. Although the task will not be formally graded, the process of producing the essay, along with the personalised feedback you will receive from your tutor, will be very useful in providing a basis for developing the skills required for the assessed assignment at the end of this book.

Note making

The skill of note making was introduced in Book 1. It is one of the steps in the active reading technique reviewed above and will be examined here with particular reference to essay writing.

You start by reflecting on the purpose of note making for essay writing.

Sometimes you will have to choose from a range of input texts about which to read first. At other times the choice will be made for you. Your essay note making begins with the case study on Nike (Text 2.1) because it is a little easier to read than the two business texts that follow.

Activity 2.9   ....

Purpose: to read and make notes on the first few paragraphs of the Nike case study text.

Task: read paragraphs 1 to 9 of Text 2.1 in Resource Book 2 and make brief notes on their content.

Be sure to keep these notes and any others you write during this session because they will all contribute to your draft essay.

This activity is discussed in the comment below.

Comment ....

The purpose of this note-making activity is, first, to introduce the content of the Nike case study and, second, to give you the opportunity to review your note-making skills.

Did you type your notes on a computer or write them by hand? If hand-written, did you write them on a separate piece of paper or around the text itself? In making notes, did you use complete sentences, whole words, abbreviations, symbols, numbers, bullet points or a mind map? Did you feel confident about how much to include or what to omit?

If you were to compare the notes you made on Text 2.1 with those made by the other students in your tutor group, you would find that – although they have much in common – no two people's notes on a given input text will be exactly the same. There will be differences in the **format** used, in the way the notes are **codified** (what combination of words, symbols and other shorthand devices are used) and, most likely, in the **selection of content** included. While some differences are to be expected, there are nevertheless several techniques which contribute to good note making. These will be examined in the following activities.

In the next activity you will consider the possible formats of notes.

Activity 2.10 ....

Purpose: to consider the different formats of notes.

Task: now read paragraphs 10 and 11 of Text 2.1 in Resource Book 2. Below there are four examples of students' notes on those paragraphs. Which format do you prefer? Can you explain why?

Extract A: Kim's notes

Outsourcing
– Advs to MNCs:
1 Low lab costs
2 Flexible JIT prod/distrib network > lower stocks req'd = costsaving
3 Preferential (a) tariffs (b) bus. legislation > facilitates factory opening/closing

Extract B: Tariq's notes

Outsourcing: Advs to MNCs = reduced wages; flexible manufacturers, suppliers, distributors = responsive JIT prod – lower stocks & assoc costs; beneficial tariffs/legislation – easier factory opening/closing.

Extract C: Rocio's notes

(See the mind map in Figure 2.3.)

Extract D: Emma's notes

The benefits to TS businesses in outsourcing production overseas include lower wages and manufacturers & distributors which are able to produce shoes 'just in time' (when market needs them & in the quantities required), which means lower stocks and associated costs. Factories can be set up & closed more easily due to advantageous tariffs & laws which TS companies seek out.

Compare your answer with that suggested in the Answer section.

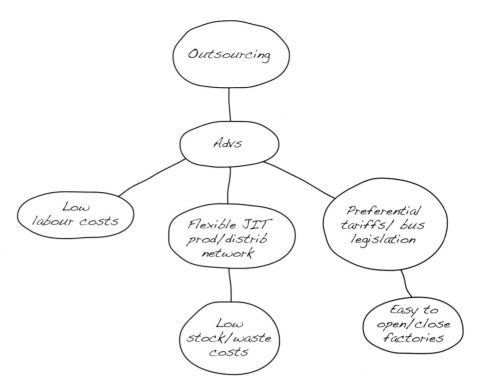

Figure 2.3 Example of a mind map for note making

Comment ....

You may have a preferred note-making format which you use all the time. Alternatively, you may find that one format is more suited to a particular source text than another. You will need to experiment with this. However, it is quite common and acceptable to combine two or more formats, as in the notes by student Jiang Li (Figure 2.4). Read paragraphs 12 to 14 of Text 2.1 in Resource Book 2 first, as they provide the basis for her note making.

Jiang Li uses a recommended note-making technique which involves a **landscape format** piece of paper, divided into three sections.

What is the **function** of each of the three sections of the notes?

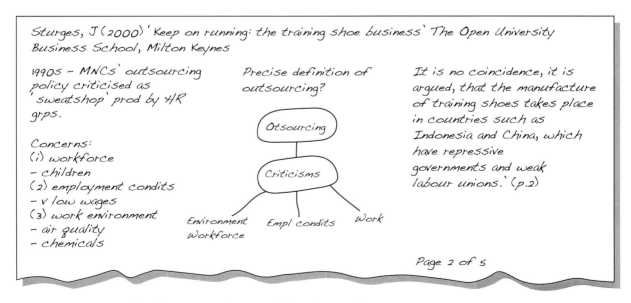

Figure 2.4 Example of a note making technique in practice

Each set of notes is headed with the full details of the source of that information. You will look more closely at the use of references in Session 6.

The first column is used for written notes on the source material (similar to those in Extracts A and B in Activity 2.10). The second column is used for your thoughts and interpretations – or **critical commentary** – on a particular section of the text. It may include comments, queries, challenges, a note on how one piece of information connects with another, or a reminder of what you want to follow up elsewhere. It can also be used for diagrams or small mind maps to help guide your understanding of the text. You could use different colours for different purposes in this column.

The third column is used for extracts taken directly from the source text. By including the page number where you found that extract, as Jiang Li has done, you will save time if you need to return to the original materials or include a quotation in your essay.

The note-making format described above can be used for either hand-written or word-processed notes.

Using abbreviated forms

Note how Extracts A to D in Activity 2.10, as well as Jiang Li's notes in Figure 2.4, include several examples of abbreviated codes (contracted words, acronyms and symbols). The use of these codes helps to keep notes brief and can speed up the note making process.

Activity 2.11

Purpose: to create a list of abbreviated codes to use in note making.

Task: look back at Extracts A and B in Activity 2.10 and Jiang Li's notes in Figure 2.4.

Prepare a table like the one below. Note down any examples of abbreviated codes in the table. Do you know what they all mean?

Check back through the notes you made for Activity 2.9. What abbreviated forms do you generally use? Add these and any further examples as you meet or think of them during your studies.

Acronym	Symbol	Contracted form
MNC (multinational corporations)		

There is no comment or suggested answer for this activity because it draws in part on your personal preferences.

You have seen that it is possible to use several formats for your note-making – either alone or in combination with one another, as shown in Figure 2.4 above.

Effective note making

In this section you will focus not on the format of notes but on how well they capture the key elements of the source text, that is to say, their **effectiveness**.

For the next activity you will read an extract from the second recommended text for this essay (Text 2.2). This extract describes a concept that will be central to your essay – the notion of **investment**. Before you start reading, take a minute or two to write down what you understand by this term in the space below.

Investment is ....

Activity 2.12 ....

Purpose: to consider which one of a selection of notes is most effective.

Task: read paragraphs 5 to 7 of Text 2.2 in Resource Book 2. When you have finished, read the four extracts of students' notes below. Which one do you think is best? What do you find problematic about each of the others?

Then compare your answers with those suggested in the Answer section.

Extract E: Juan's notes

Economists gen consider high investment = healthier econ. Relationship between investment levels & econ performance.

Defin of investment: part of company spending used to expand & replace capital. Capital = things that are not consumed but create more income. eg spending on premises, new machinery, associated staff training etc.

Investment > gains to some/all company stakeholders. In private sector = higher profits/more shares. In public sector = cheaper, improved customer services.

Extract F: Hussein's notes

Investment = economic performance.

Investment = capital eg land, building, equipment – not used every day.

Investment in eg private sector > higher profits/share prices; in eg private sector > better services.

Extract G: Sofia's notes

Pos rel betw levels of investment & economic perf.

Inv = company's capital spending > fut returns for stakeholders: ie

1. profit/share rises – priv sect. 2. improved user services – publ/NP sect.

Extract H: Anna's notes

Investment = important concept. Economists gen agree high investment levels assoc'd w/healthy econ ie apparent link betw level of investm & gen econ perf.

> Investm = part of firm's spending which increases/replenishes capital stock. Capital = company purchases not immed used up in firm's e/day operations, retained to generate fut inc. eg cost of land/premises; purch of new equipt/assoc'd training.
>
> Investm > generation of fut reward/benef for sh/holders. Private sector = increased profit/share value; public/non-profit sector – better/more cost effective client/community services.

Comment

These examples of note making show the variety of ways of capturing information from the same text. Extract G is an example of good note making in that it identifies the key information of the source text and captures it concisely.

The other three examples are less successful. Did you establish the reasons why?

Extract E is too **long and wordy**. The main reason is that it does not distinguish between the key information in the source text – which should be included – and the less important details – which can be omitted. Instead it includes almost the entire original. A further contribution to the length and wordiness of this extract is that the notes include very few abbreviated forms.

Extract F is unsuccessful in that it is not entirely **accurate**. Here the problem is that the source materials have not been processed with sufficient attention and understanding. The result is notes which are at times vague or incorrect.

The main problem with Extract H is that it is composed of many of the same words as the original. When making notes, it is important to avoid using too many of the words of the source text, as there is the risk that – when used as the basis of your essay – the result will contain identical strings of words as the original. This is discussed in more detail in the sections on **plagiarism** in Sessions 4 and 5.

Brevity, accuracy and careful wording are three important elements of good note making.

You may recall the method for making notes from Book 1. You should begin by identifying the high-level generalisations in each section that you read. The next step is to compress these generalisations into as few words as possible, by reducing them to their key concepts, by changing verbs into noun groups, by using symbols and abbreviations and by leaving out non-essential words such as 'a' and 'the'.

For example, Figure 2.4 shows how Jiang Li reduces the original source text (Text 2.1, paragraph 12):

> In the early 1990s, the leading training shoe companies' strategy of using low-cost Asian labour to manufacture their products came under increasing scrutiny from human rights groups. By the end of the decade, campaign groups aimed at stamping out this so-called 'sweatshop' production were active in the USA, the UK and Australia.

to the following condensed notes:

1990s – MNCs' outsourcing policy criticised as 'sweatshop' prod by HR grps.

Mapping and framing

Having looked at the different **formats** of notes and what makes notes **effective**, this section considers the different **purposes** for which notes are used.

Book 1 introduced the distinction between **mapping** a text – to get an overview of its content – and **framing** it – to focus on the text from a particular perspective. Note making may be used for either purpose. **Mapping** requires you to capture the key content of each section of the **whole** text in brief note form. In contrast, **framing** involves reading the text from a particular angle, looking for specific answers. Therefore, your notes will be organised with such a framework in mind.

The purpose of the note making that you did on Text 2.1 is to **map** this case study text. However, because special attention has been given to aspects of the note making process, the resulting notes may be more detailed than those required for an overview of a source text. The next activity completes the task of mapping Text 2.1.

Activity 2.13 ....

Purpose: to complete the mapping of a source text.

Task: now read paragraphs 15 to 19 of Text 2.1 in Resource Book 2. Make notes using the three-column technique described in Activity 2.10. Focus on each paragraph in turn. Identify the high-level generalisations in each one and condense these into brief notes using noun phrases and abbreviated forms in column one. In column two note your comments and queries on the text and draw mind maps or diagrams if helpful. Use column three for any quotations from the text that you think could be relevant.

There is no suggested answer for this activity because you will produce your own version of notes on this text.

Text 2.1 was a case study on Nike. You will now consider Texts 2.2 and 2.3. As mentioned above, Text 2.2 is part of an Open University business course. It outlines the business concepts that are relevant to this essay title. You have already made notes on one section of the text, which focused on the concept of *investment*.

Text 2.2 also acts as an introduction to Text 2.3, which is an extract from a more theoretical article covering some of the same concepts.

Texts 2.2 and 2.3 are the explanation texts – those which provide a frame through which the **evidence** in Text 2.1 can be interpreted. Texts 2.2 and 2.3 include some important, and perhaps challenging, business concepts. It is important that you take time to understand them, as they will be central to your response to essay title B. The main focus of the texts is the concept of an *economy*. Before you start reading, write down what you understand by this term:

An economy ....

....

....

The following activities will help you process the content of Texts 2.2 and 2.3. We suggest you use the three-column note-making format for this purpose, heading each set of notes with the title of each source.

Activity 2.14   ....

Purpose: to read and make notes on Texts 2.2 and 2.3 in preparation for your essay.

Task 1: read paragraphs 1 and 2 of Text 2.2 in Resource Book 2. These introduce the business notion of an *economy* – which you have identified as a key concept in your essay title.

Now turn to Text 2.3 which explains the concept of *economy* in more detail. Read the complete text carefully, making brief but careful notes to map its four paragraphs, paying particular attention to the different *agents* which contribute to an economy and how they are connected in the model of the *circular flow of income*. You may want to draw your own version of an explanatory diagram to complement your notes.

When you have finished, check your understanding of the text by answering the following questions.

(a) What are the main flows of income **to organisations** from: (i) households; (ii) banks; (iii) the government?

(b) What are the main payments **from organisations** to: (i) households; (ii) banks; (iii) the government?

(c) Two types of **organisations** are mentioned. What is the difference between them?

Now compare your answers with those in the Answer section.

Task 2: earlier you read about an important business concept which will be central to your essay – *investment*.

Now read paragraphs 3 and 4 of Text 2.2. These introduce the key concept of *investment.* This will be a central idea in your essay. You read and made notes on paragraphs 5 to 7 earlier. Make sure you attach those notes to the set you make on these readings. Now read the section on investment again. You will see that there is an additional paragraph – paragraph 8 – which you have not yet made notes on. Read this carefully, paying particular attention to what is meant by the *multiplier effect*, and add notes on this to your original document.

Task 3: paragraphs 9 and 10 of Text 2.2 look at the four indicators of a country's economic health. These are also central to your essay. Read this section and make notes on each indicator. Finally, read paragraphs 11 and 12 and make notes on those too.

There is no suggested answer for Tasks 2 and 3 because you will produce your own version of notes on these readings.

Comment ....

Although challenging, your reading and note making in this activity represent a valuable contribution to your consideration of essay title B, '*Discuss the extent to which a large corporation such as Nike might influence the economic health of a developing country*'.

Earlier you established that this essay requires your views on the **causal relationship** between the activity of large corporations and the economic health of developing countries.

As mentioned earlier, the two business texts (Texts 2.2 and 2.3) are **explanatory** texts, in that they provide a **frame** for interpreting the Nike case study (Text 2.1), which represents real world evidence.

Therefore, the next step is to review some of the explanatory concepts that you have recently met in the business texts and reflect on how they might be applied to such evidence.

For the next activity you need to assemble the notes you made on the three source texts that you have read in this session.

Activity 2.15 ....

Purpose: to re-read an evidence-type text through an explanatory framework.

Task: re-read the notes you made on the two business texts (Texts 2.2 and 2.3), taking care to ensure that their content is clear to you. If you have any doubts, return to the original texts to clarify them.

Now read the notes you made on the Nike case study (Text 2.1). Using the concepts from the two business texts as a frame for your reading, make a brief summary or map of the central themes of the essay, including definitions and examples where possible.

The following key concepts may help you in this.

Cause	Effect
MNCs	Developing countries

Economy: (i) economic agents; (ii) circular flow of income; (iii) a healthy economy; (iv) investment; (v) multiplier effect

MNCs' policy of outsourcing production:
    Positive effects on economic health of developing countries
    Negative effects on economic health of developing countries

There is no suggested answer for this activity because you will produce your own version of the output task.

Reviewing your mind map

Activity 2.16 ....

Purpose: to review your brainstorming mind map after reading the three source texts.

Task: look back at the mind map you drew in Activity 2.6. This encapsulated the initial ideas and questions that you generated around the key concepts in the essay title. How has your reading of the source texts developed these ideas? How far has it answered your questions? How might you develop it in the light of the new knowledge you have gained?

Choose one key concept from your original mind map and extend it by adding any newly gained information, answers to the questions that you initially posed and links between ideas as appropriate.

There is no suggested answer for this activity because you will develop your own unique mind map.

Comment ....

Your brainstorming mind map represents a starting point for the development of your ideas for your essay. The aim of reading and making notes on the source texts is to build on this state of knowledge. The fact that you can connect the new knowledge captured in your notes with your initial mind map demonstrates that learning has happened since you began considering the essay title.

2.5 Step 4: Outlining the essay

Taking a position

You may recall that essay title B asked you to give **your** opinion on the amount of influence large corporations might have on the economic health of developing countries. Your task has been to identify the different forms such influence takes, how significant these forms are, and whether they are positive, negative or a mixture of both.

Perhaps you started out with very little knowledge about the key concepts in the essay title. You will have raised several questions both before and during your reading of the source texts. Through your reading you will have accumulated considerable information and extended your knowledge further.

You might have set out with a particular viewpoint on the topic to be discussed. Your reading may have provided you with evidence to reinforce and support this view. On the other hand, you may have gained an alternative perspective on the issue and changed your initial ideas somewhat. The essay preparation process is a dynamic one in which you will constantly assess and reassess your position as regards the essay title and your reading around it.

You should now have a comprehensive set of notes and ideas about the essay title. The next step is to start organising these into an essay **outline**.

An outline is a broad 'map' of the content and sequencing of an essay. It usually takes the form of a series of headings, each of which may be accompanied by sub-headings or brief references to evidence or examples. These should be in the order in which they will appear in the essay.

When making notes, you spend a lot of time reducing many pages of reading to a few words. This is a very useful note-making process. You can also make an outline out of key concepts like this. When you write a list of key concepts and organise them into groups, you have a good basis for an essay. However, as you will see in Session 3, it is also important to make points in your essay. One danger when you write a key concept outline is that you know **what you are going to write about**, you just don't really know **what you are going to write about it**. If you write a point-based outline, you are already thinking about what your essay will say. In the next activity, you will compare a key concept-based outline with a point-based one.

Activity 2.17 ....

Purpose: to compare two kinds of essay outline.

Task 1: read Text 2.4 in Resource Book 2, which is a key-concept-based outline for an essay you studied in Session 1. Then read Text 2.5, which is a point-based outline for the same essay. Do you agree that the point-based outline will probably be more useful than the key concept-based one?

Task 2: the final three sections of the point-based outline are not complete (F, G and Conclusion). Look at the last three paragraphs of the essay in Extract 2.6. What points do you think the student could have included in the outline they prepared for this essay?

Compare your answers with those suggested in the Answer section.

Comment ....

The difference between a concept-based and a point-based outline is that the latter shows what you intend to say about the concepts and topics in your outline. In the example you looked at, many of the points are cause–effect points. They show that the reason a concept is in the outline is that it has a business impact which explains why Nike is the biggest training shoe company in the world. It shows what the writer will say about the question in the title.

In writing an outline, it is not always possible to be as detailed as in this example. However, the more you are able to start thinking about the argument structure in the essay outline, the clearer the argument should eventually be in the essay.

Activity 2.18 ....

Purpose: to produce an outline essay based on essay title B.

Task: using the notes you have compiled in this session, write an essay outline on essay title B: 'Discuss the extent to which a large corporation such as Nike might influence the economic health of a developing country.'

There is no suggested answer for this activity. However, your outline will be used as the basis of the draft of your essay, as explained below.

Writing your first draft

Now that you have drawn up an essay outline, the next step is to write the first draft of your essay. This should present the points of your essay in more detail, using full sentences and paragraphs.

There is no set method for writing the first draft of an essay. Some people write by following their outline from the beginning to the end. Others prefer to start elsewhere, writing up each section in a less regular order, until the whole text is complete.

We would prefer you to approach this first draft in your own way, drawing on your previous experience of essay writing and on what you have learned in this book so far. Therefore, there are no further instructions at this point. Session 3 will help you reflect on what you have produced, as will the personalised feedback that you will receive from your tutor.

Activity 2.19 ....

Purpose: to produce a draft essay.

Task: drawing on the input texts that you have processed and the outline you have devised, write a first draft of essay title B: 'Discuss the extent to which a large corporation such as Nike might influence the economic health of a developing country'.

When you have finished, send your draft essay to your tutor by email. It should be accompanied by the outline that you wrote for this essay in Activity 2.18.

2.6 Critical reflection

You have practised several skills in this session. The following questions will help you reflect on what you have learned.

How useful have you found this introduction to the processes involved in preparing to write an essay? Which section(s) did you find most helpful?

What did you find most difficult? Why do you think this was?

How confident do you feel about the following? (Use a scoring system from 1 to 4, where 1 is not confident and 4 is very confident):

Analysing an essay title

Selecting appropriate source materials

The relationship between sources of **evidence** and **explanation**

Note-making techniques

In what ways has your knowledge on the impact of multinational companies on developing countries changed through the reading associated with this session?

Use the online Learning Journal for your personal reflection.

2.7 Review

In this session you have been introduced to the processes involved in preparing to write an essay. In particular you should have:

- analysed an essay title to be clear about its requirements, and brainstormed ideas for its content
- learned about managing source materials in an essay and applied active reading and note-making techniques to three texts
- used your notes as the basis of an essay outline
- written your first draft of an essay.

2.8 Answer section

Activity 2.1

(A) *Explain* is an instruction word.

(B) *Discuss* is an instruction word; *a large corporation such as Nike* is an example of scope.

Activity 2.2

The key concepts are: *large corporation, economic health* and *a developing country*.

Activity 2.3

Task 1:	other examples of MNCs include Coca-Cola, Pepsi, McDonalds, Microsoft.
Task 2:	a healthy balance of payments, high employment, stable prices, low inflation, high (or rising) living standards.
Task 3	
(a)	Examples of developing countries include: Vietnam, China, Indonesia, Peru, Bhutan, Ghana.
(b)	Features of developing countries include: a relatively low standard of living; a low per capita income; limited industrial development.
(c)	**Developing countries:** underdeveloped countries; undeveloped countries; non-industrialised nations; the Third World; the Majority World; the South; LEDCs (less economically developed countries).
	Developed countries: industrialised nations; the West; western countries; MEDCs (more economically developed countries).

Activity 2.4

A Explain why Nike is the biggest training shoe company in the world.	
1 Why is Nike the biggest training shoe company in the world?	✓
2 Is Nike the biggest training shoe company in the world?	✗
3 How has Nike become the biggest training shoe company in the world?	✓
4 In what ways is Nike the biggest training shoe company in the world?	✗
5 What are the reasons behind Nike's success?	✓

Activity 2.5

Discuss <u>the extent</u> to which a large corporation such as Nike <u>might</u> influence the economic health of a developing country.

Activity 2.7

You may have listed any of the following techniques from the active reading method introduced in Book 1.

(a) Pre-reading activities

- Be clear what output you want from reading the text.
- Before you read carefully, look quickly through the text to see what it is generally about (good places to look are: title, introduction, beginning sentences of each paragraph, final paragraph).
- Draw a mind map of some of the knowledge you already have about the content.
- Think of a question that the text will answer for you before you read it.

(b) During reading activities

- Keep asking more questions during reading.
- Read the text carefully, trying to note how it is organised.
- Underline **high levels** in the text.
- Write notes on the text.

(c) Post-reading activities

- Write notes somewhere else, not on the text.
- If possible, draw mind maps.
- Produce a summary.

Activity 2.8

Texts 2, 6, 7, 8 and 9 are likely to be more relevant.

Activity 2.10

Extracts A, B, C and D represent four distinct note-making formats.

Extract A is organised in the form of a hierarchical system of headings, numbers and letters.

Extract B is a series of condensed sentences.

Extract C is a mind map, which provides a visual representation of the content and the way its elements interrelate. This kind of mind mapping has a different function from the brainstorming you did in Activity 2.6, in which you noted down your own thoughts, questions and ideas about the essay title.

Extract D is different from A, B and C in that it is not an example of note making but rather an example of **paraphrasing**. Note making condenses the original text into as brief a form as possible; paraphrasing uses full sentences and different wording to **rewrite** the original. Although paraphrasing has its uses, it has a different function from note making and cannot be compared to A, B and C, each of which is an effective note-making format.

Activity 2.12

Extract E is too long and wordy; F is inaccurate; G is an example of good notes; H has too many words taken from the original text.

Activity 2.14

Task 1

(a) (i) consumer spending; (ii) loans; (iii) grants and other types of support.

(b) (i) wages; (ii) loan repayments; (iii) taxes.

(c) One type of organisation produces consumer goods. The other produces machinery and raw materials for those organisations.

Activity 2.17

Task 2

F Innovation – business and technological
Nike outsource manufacturing/South East Asia – reducing the need for capital investment in factories and equipment.

Human rights complaints in factories → 'corporate responsibility' as opportunity for innovation and leadership.

G Innovation – design and technology
Tom Vanderbilt quote, 'design = consumer appeal'.

Evidence is that Nike tripled design budget since 1995.

Nike led way in technological advances in the training shoe market – e.g. pockets of pressurised gas and waffle sole designs.

Conclusion
Understood environment to produce quality, affordable products and market requirements to sell millions of shoes.

SESSION **3 The design of an essay**

3.1 Introduction

Session 1 introduced the general features of a business studies essay. Session 2 outlined the essay-writing process. This session looks more closely at the design of an essay. It focuses on the first two successful essay characteristics from the list in Session 1. You may recall that these were:

- relevance to the title
- a reasoned argument
- the use of source texts
- appropriate presentation.

Session 2 and this session form a pair. The essay production flow chart in Figure 3.1 illustrates this. In Session 2 you practised reading, thinking and writing processes, using inputs for an essay about Nike and developing countries. You also began to produce some

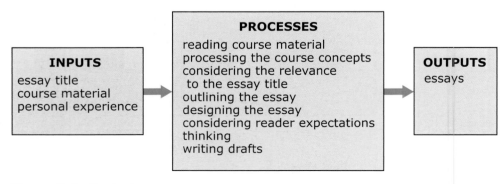

Figure 3.1 Producing an essay

outputs which were still rough products – notes, outlines and first drafts. In Session 3, you will concentrate on the final product – the essay.

Successful essays are essays that are fit for purpose. They are designed to succeed. Every time a student writes an essay, they create a new product – and it is important that they do this. However, while every essay is a new product, essays are not all completely different. This is why they are all called 'essays'.

The idea of this course is that you can learn a lot from studying how essays are designed. However, the reason for looking at the design of other essays is not to copy them. It is to be inspired and encouraged by them. In the end, each time you write an essay, you will have to use your understanding of essay design **to make a new design**.

The design process begins early and the final design may already be clear to you when you first see an essay title. However, it is more likely that the design develops as you go through the processes you practised in Session 2. Eventually, your design will be obvious in the finished product – your essay.

Learning outcomes

In this session you will look at examples of students' assignments in order to:

- become familiar with the design of some essays
- develop further understanding of argument in an essay
- learn ways of managing information and linking ideas in an argument
- practise writing skills to develop an argument that is relevant to the essay title.

3.2 How do essays develop professional communication skills?

People do not write essays in their workplace. Essay writing is an academic activity. So it is important to address the question, how do essays develop professional communication skills?

The short answer is that essays develop the skill of argument. Workplace writing might seem to be much more about reporting facts and much less about argument but that is wrong. Book 3 is about workplace writing and is called *Producing Influential Documents* because workplace writing is writing that persuades people.

One of the best ways to develop the skill of writing persuasively is to practise essay writing. A successful essay, as you have already seen, has a convincing and a coherent argument. In Book 3, you will learn how to adapt your writing style to the different purposes of workplace documents. The skills you develop in this book on writing successful argument essays will give you the basis of successful workplace writing.

What is an argument?

Arguments are made up of two main elements: **claims** and **basis**.

For example, a claim might be: 'I doubt that large corporations such as Nike influence the economic health of a developing country'.

To make this claim convincing, there needs to be a basis for it. In an argument essay, there are two main kinds of basis.

1   Business studies concepts, models and theories which explain how the business world works. An example is the circular flow model of the economy.

2   Facts, figures and reports which are data or evidence from the world of business. An example is the Nike case study.

Successful argument essays bring **claims, evidence** and **explanations** together in a convincing text. In this session you will study how they do that.

3.3 Essay design

In Session 2 you practised the skills that you need to process an essay title and produce an essay outline and a first draft. In this session you will look at several essays written by business students in response to the same essay title. These essays were judged to be successful by their tutors. You will explore what makes them successful and, more generally, what they show about professional communication. The focus is on how the design of these essays meets the requirements of the situation. These are texts that are fit for their purpose.

Activity 3.1   ....

Purpose: to revise the characteristics of a successful essay.

Task: look at the essay outline or draft you produced at the end of Session 2. How well does it meet the four criteria for a successful essay listed at the beginning of this session? Be specific: for each criterion, find an example in your text which you think meets it.

Comment   ....

Sometimes it is difficult to say **exactly** why a text is – or is not – successful. It is often easier to make general comments, such as, 'There is something wrong with the argument here' or 'This seems very relevant'. However, this is a course on developing communication skills, so it is not enough to make just general comments.

This is why this course introduces a checklist of criteria for successful communication in essays. This checklist is based on the study of many successful essays. As you know, the whole checklist is in the Appendix at the end of the book. In Session 2, you looked in particular at the set of criteria for dealing with how to use source material. In this session, you will look at the second set of criteria in the checklist, which is called 'Structure and development of the text'. It is a set of criteria for evaluating how successful the argument of an essay is. Some of the criteria may not be clear at the moment but they are explored further during this session.

> **Box 3.1   Criteria for evaluating the argument of an essay**
>
> **B   *Structure and development of the text – is the structure and development of the essay clear and appropriate to the title and its context?***
>
> 1   Text structure is appropriate to the task
> 2   Beginning of the essay introduces the argument
> 3   Beginnings of paragraphs and sentences are orientated to the argument
> 4   Argument moves between high-level generalisations and lower-level details and examples
> 5   Claims build up the argument
> 6   Evidence is used that supports the claims in the argument
> 7   Explanations link the evidence to the claims
> 8   Information flow in the argument is linked and connected
> 9   Statement of conclusion follows from argument and relates to title
>
> Source: adapted from materials created by Helen Bonano and Janet Jones, MASUS Project, University of Sydney, 1997.

Beginning and end

The simplest thing you can say about an essay is that it has a beginning, a middle and an end. Although this sounds obvious, it is still important. For many reasons, your reader needs to know which part of your essay they are in – and so do you. The next activity looks at the beginning and the end of a successful essay.

Activity 3.2 ....

Purpose: to identify where the introduction to an essay ends and the conclusion begins.

Task: Text 3.1 in Resource Book 2 is Amina's essay in response to the title you processed in Session 2: 'Discuss the extent to which a large corporation such as Nike might influence the economic health of a developing country.'

Identify where the introduction to Amina's essay ends and where the conclusion begins. Write down exactly why you think this. For this activity, you **do not** need to read the whole essay carefully.

Compare your answer with that suggested in the Answer section.

Comment ....

The student who wrote this essay had more time and information to write it than you had for your outline and draft in Session 2. How does it compare with yours? To answer this question, the next activity looks a little more closely at what Amina wrote in the introduction.

Reading an introduction

Introductions are important for readers. Good introductions tell the reader what to expect in the essay and strongly influence how they understand the essay. The next activity looks more closely at what Amina's introduction tells her readers.

Activity 3.3

Purpose: to read and understand a successful essay introduction.

Task: read each statement in the table below and then decide whether Amina included these ideas in the introduction to her essay (not necessarily in the same words). If she has, tick the second column. If not, tick the third column. In the fourth column, write down the actual words from the introduction which Amina uses.

Statement	In Amina's introduction	Not in Amina's introduction	Words in the introduction
1 Large corporations do not influence the countries they are in.			
2 The impact of large corporations in developing countries is less than in developed countries.			
3 The Nike indicator shows a link between business activities and standards of living.			
4 Investment is one of the four indicators of economic health.			
5 Investment by multinational corporations in developing countries is more positive than negative.			

Compare your answers with those suggested in the Answer section.

Comment

In her introduction, Amina makes several clear statements about her essay and the argument she will present. These statements manage the way her reader will understand her essay. When people communicate they always try to make sense of what they hear or read. Even when the communication is difficult or unclear, people still try to make sense of it. This is what humans do – they communicate. Only when they decide the communication is actually nonsense will they give up trying to make sense of it.

So in the situation in Figure 3.2, the listener at the bus stop will start by trying to make sense of the speaker's three statements by linking them together in some way.

One way of linking these three separate statements is with an introductory statement. If the speaker started by saying, 'I've got so much to do this afternoon', she would tell the listener what the three following statements are about. The listener would have a frame and could make sense of what he hears. Because the speaker does not make the frame clear, the listener will try to make his own frame.

Figure 3.2 Communicating meaning (Source: adapted from Giltrow, 1995, p. 115)

For example, he might make a link between the insurance document and the child's toothache – perhaps the toothache is an injury and the insurance will pay for treatment. If these links between statements don't seem to work, in the end the listener will give up and decide the speaker does not know what they are talking about.

Exactly the same can happen in writing. Readers want to make sense of your writing. Your purpose is to control the way they do this. If you don't make clear to them what the meaning is, they will still make some kind of sense out of it. The introduction is an important place to make your meaning clear. Just as the statement 'I've got so much to do this afternoon' tells the listener what the following statements are about, the introduction to an essay tells the reader what the essay is about. An introduction is much more important in writing than in speaking because the reader cannot ask the writer to explain their meaning. As you saw in Session 1, writing is less dependent on the immediate context and the reader has to work hard on their own to interpret what the writing is about.

The design of an introduction

The **introduction** comes at the beginning of the essay. It sets the scene, introduces the reader to the argument of the essay and indicates how it will be developed. You can examine how Amina designed her introduction to do this in the next activity.

Activity 3.4 ....

Purpose: to recognise how an introduction works.

Task: Amina's introduction is reproduced in Extract A. The table below it lists five of the main functions of an introduction. Find the words in Amina's introduction that perform each of these functions. They may not be in the same order as in the table.

Extract A

Discuss the extent to which a large corporation such as Nike might influence the economic health of a developing country.

[S1] Wherever a large corporation such as Nike operates, the scale of its activity will have an effect on the locality. [S2] In a developing country, this activity might have a significant influence on the whole economy of the area. [S3] Economic commentators refer to 'the Nike indicator', assuming a clear link 'between the companies' business activities in Asian countries and the subsequent rise in those countries' standards of living' (Sturges, 2000, p. 12). [S4] This essay will look at how much, and in which way, the business activities of a large corporation might influence the health of the economy in a developing country. [S5] It begins with an explanation of the terms 'economy' and 'investment' and then goes on to consider four indicators of economic health. [S6] Although multinational corporations' investment in developing countries is beneficial for such countries, there are some negative impacts as well.

Function	Which words perform these functions?
Link back to the title	
Give a general background to the topic	
Identify the key concepts in the essay	
State the essay's central argument or claim	
Say how the essay will be organised	

Compare your answers with those suggested in the Answer section.

Comment ....

Amina creates a context for her essay title by writing about the general effects of Nike in developing countries (sentences 1 to 3). Her main argument or **central claim** is that large corporations – through their investments – can have both positive and negative impacts on the economy of a developing country (sentence 6). Amina provides a brief outline of the development of her essay: her essay will assess the impact of large corporations on the economic health of a developing country by considering economic factors (sentence 5). She uses key concepts from the title to link back to the title and some additional key concepts that point forwards towards the argument in the essay.

The design of the introduction to Amina's essay can be visually represented as a funnel (Figure 3.3).

The funnel diagram shows that the introduction leads into the essay by narrowing down the main claim of the argument. However, this main claim is actually a high-level generalisation. It is there to give the reader a view across the essay. They will use it to make sense of the argument in the rest of the essay. So the introduction can also be seen as steps down from high-level generalisation towards the lower-level details in the rest of the essay. This can be shown in a step diagram (Figure 3.4).

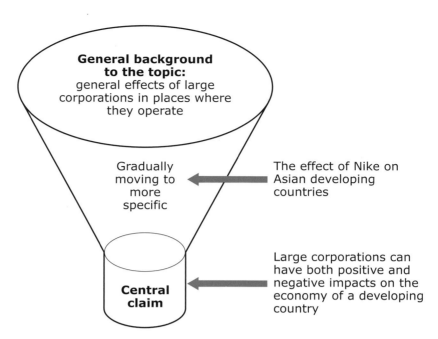

Figure 3.3 Funnel-like view of the structure of an introduction (Source: adapted from Oshima and Hogue, 2006, p. 60)

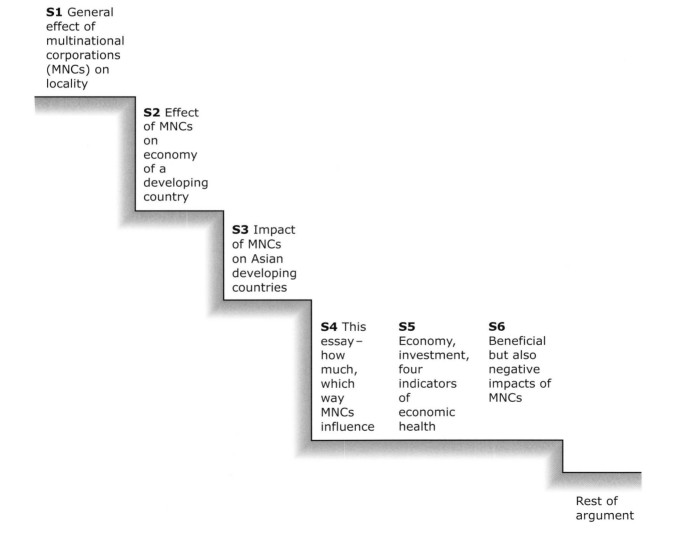

Figure 3.4 The levels in an introduction

It is crucial to get your essay introduction right. When the reader stands on the high level of the introduction they should be able to see across the argument in the rest of the text. The introduction communicates what the essay is **about**.

Activity 3.5 ....

Purpose: to reinforce your awareness of how an introduction presents a high-level generalisation or claim.

Task: Extracts B and C below are two more introductions to the same essay assignment as Extract A. For each one underline the high-level generalisation that is the central claim of the essay. Which claim is most similar to the one in Amina's introduction? Write down your reasons for your decision.

Extract B

Discuss the extent to which a large corporation such as Nike might influence the economic health of a developing country.

Multinational corporations (MNCs), like Nike, operate – seemingly regardless of geographical boundaries – to reduce costs, widen their market and increase profits. Developing countries feature in this process because they offer cheap labour. Their economic health is often affected considerably by investment from MNCs. China, Taiwan and Korea have seen a gradual economic growth but only because they embraced this investment and the global environment. This paper argues that the extent to which MNCs influence the economic health of a developing country is dependent on that country's response to the corporation.

Extract C

Discuss the extent to which a large corporation such as Nike might influence the economic health of a developing country.

I am going to look at what a large corporation is and determine what economic health means as well as what a developing country might look like. Further I will look at aggregate demand, and measurement of economic performance. Arguably, large corporations support development and economic growth in developing countries, but is there evidence that corporate growth and corporate malpractice can produce disadvantage?

Compare your answers with those suggested in the Answer section.

Comment ....

Both introductions make a central claim which is an overview of the argument in the essay. If you can do this in your introduction you are taking very firm control over your reader's understanding of your essay. From this point on, your reader will have two questions in mind:

• Why does this writer claim this?

• How will they show me this claim is true?

Once your reader asks those questions, you can be sure that you have started an argument essay.

Making a claim in the opening paragraph is so powerful that not everyone can do it. Very often when a writer begins to write they are not completely sure what the main claim of their essay is. Often they can only see it clearly after they have finished the essay. In that situation, it is a good idea to go back to the introduction and add the central claim afterwards.

In the next activity, you will practise adding information to introductions which have parts missing.

Activity 3.6

Purpose: to reinforce your understanding of the work that an introduction does in framing an essay.

Task: Extracts D to G below are four more introductions. Four sets of sentences have been removed from the introductions and are listed below the extracts. Decide which introduction each sentence comes from and where it belongs in that introduction. Decide what functions the sentences perform (use the list of functions from Activity 3.4).

Extract D

[S1] In answering this question, I will seek to briefly explain what an economy is and what performance indicators and models can be applied to assess the health of an economy. [S2] I will go on to identify some of the key influences that multinational companies like Nike can bring to bear on developing economies and the effect this has had on countries trying to improve the state of their economic wealth.

Extract E

[S1] Phil Knight founded Nike in 1972 in America. [S2] Over the past thirty years Nike has developed into one of the most influential global corporations of our times. [S3] One of the strategies that Nike has employed and which has played a large part in ensuring its success is that of outsourcing the production of training shoes to independent countries in South East Asia where labour costs are much lower. [S4] This is a trend that most training shoe companies have eventually followed. [S5] Furthermore, there are many large corporations that have taken their production, or simply expanded, into developing countries. [S6] With this move into developing countries, one must ask just how far large corporations, such as Nike, influence the economic health of the countries in question. [S7] To what extent do they affect their economic health? [S8] Are there distinct advantages and disadvantages and does one outweigh the other?

Extract F

[S1] In this assignment I'll define the term 'economy' and what's meant by a 'healthy' and 'unhealthy' economy. [S2] I'll draw a comparison between Nike's influence and that of other large organisations who outsource parts of their business to developing countries.

Extract G

[S1] A developing country can be defined as one with a low per capita income by world standards. [S2] Most people within the country will have relatively low standards of living and less access to goods and services than people in higher-income countries. [S3] Healthy economies are usually relatively stable and perform well in the four most commonly used indicators; unemployment rates, economic growth rate or Real Gross Domestic Product (Real GDP), rate of inflation and the balance of payments.

Missing sentences

(a) I'll provide an overview of the circular flow of income model and the multiplier effect and use these models to examine the extent to which a large corporation such as Nike might influence the economic health of a developing country.

(b) This essay will attempt to explore the impact that could occur within the economy of a developing country when influenced by a large corporation such as Nike and consider how far-reaching those effects might be.

(c) In this essay I will define what is meant by 'a healthy economy'. I will introduce a model used to analyse the relationships found in economies. I will then look at the influence of large corporations, such as Nike, on developing countries, assessing whether they have a positive influence or a negative influence on the economic health of the developing countries concerned.

(d) I will argue that investment by large corporations can provide significant benefits to the state's economic health and wealth, which albeit often inequitably shared, can directly improve the life of its citizens.

Compare your answers with those suggested in the Answer section.

Comment

Successful essays are not all the same. Not all introductions include the five functions you have been looking at. For example, sometimes students do not include a central claim in their introduction, possibly because they are not sure what their argument will be when they start writing. Writing an essay is a way of learning: what you know by the end of the essay is not the same as what you know at the beginning. For this reason, in your introduction, you may just write what you will do in your essay but not include what your argument will be.

However, it is important to remember that your essay is also communication. Just because you know how the parts of your essay fit together, it does not mean your reader does. You have already seen in the case of the incoherent speaker at the bus stop that, if you don't give your reader a strong frame in the introduction, they may not understand you. This is true for any text. Professional communicators must always make decisions about the most effective way to design the text. If you see your essay as professional communication, and you want your reader to understand you, it is worth considering putting your central claim in the introduction.

Designing the argument

In Session 2, you identified several concepts and models in two business studies texts in preparation for writing a draft of this essay. In this section, you look at how other students used these concepts and models to design the argument in their essays.

Activity 3.7   ....

Purpose: to recall relevant concepts and models for this essay as preparation for reading some example essays.

Task: without looking back at your notes, make a mind map, or write a list, of the concepts and models you identified in the business studies texts you read in Session 2.

Compare your answers with those suggested in the Answer section.

Comment   ....

As pointed out in Session 2, these concepts and models should provide the basis for the claims you make in your essay. In the next activity you look at whether Amina uses them in her essay to explain the claim she makes in her introduction.

Activity 3.8   ....

Purpose: to see which concepts and models from the source material a student has used in their essay.

Task 1: scan through Text 3.1 and mark all the places where Amina refers to the source material she has used. To do this, look for her references to authors' names (these are usually in brackets).

Task 2: now, tick the places where Amina refers to the business studies texts, rather than the case study material. (The business studies texts will usually be the source of the concepts she uses.)

Task 3: look at the list of concepts in the answer to Activity 3.7. In Amina's essay, underline any of these concepts that she uses.

Comment   ....

From paragraph 2 to paragraph 7, Amina has used the concepts from her reading to write her essay. These concepts are the high-level viewing platforms that organise the text. When you underline these concepts you produce a map of the text. They are essential for the essay. However, the success of the essay depends on how these concepts are used in the argument.

To investigate this, you will look at Amina's argument using a communications model. In many ways this model shows how all professional communication works.

As you have already learned, an argument consists of three main parts as shown in Figure 3.5.

You already know that Amina has a central claim in her introduction and has used several concepts in the body of her essay. In the next activity you look at how these make an argument.

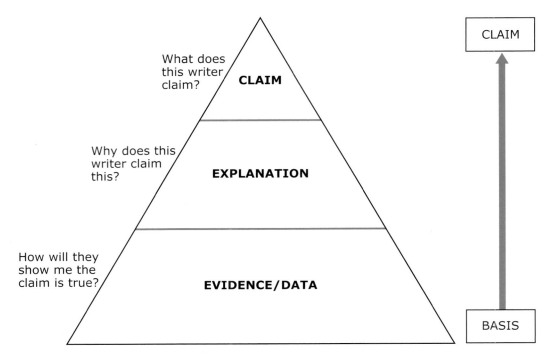

Figure 3.5   A model of argument structure

Activity 3.9   ....

Purpose: to begin reading Amina's essay in order to understand her argument, focusing on paragraph 2.

Task 1: read paragraph 2 of Amina's essay and label Figure 3.6 (a), (b) and (c). (Note the direction of the arrows.) For (a) you should write a title for the diagram.

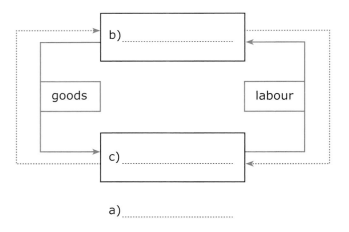

Figure 3.6   Diagram for use with Activity 3.9

Task 2: paragraph 2 describes what happens if there is an increase in the demand for one of the resources in Figure 3.6. Which resource is it? Why might demand for it increase? What will happen if demand for it increases?

Task 3: use what you have read in paragraph 2 to complete the following sentences.

Data	Nike is Vietnam's biggest employer.
Claim	This means that ...
Explanation	Because ...

Task 4: use the sentences from Task 3 to write a short paragraph. Organise the sentences in the order given below and use the words given to show how the steps in the argument are linked and connected.

Claim	
Data	since
Explanation	This is because

Task 5: in Tasks 3 and 4 you organised the claim, the data and the explanation in two different sequences. What sequence does Amina use to organise them in her paragraph?

Compare your answers with those suggested in the Answer section.

Comment   ....

In this activity you have worked with one paragraph of Amina's essay. However, this paragraph plays a part in the argument of the essay. It makes its own mini-argument, complete with a claim, data and an explanation. Argument essays are usually made up of mini-arguments like this which provide a basis for the central claim or main argument. This is why it is usually a good idea to make your central claim clear in the introduction. There will be many ideas in your essay and, as your reader moves through them, they will use your central claim to remind them what your essay is actually about.

You have also seen that you can put the claim, the data and the explanation in different orders. Again this depends on what your central claim is and what you are trying to achieve. This essay is about the economic health of a country; Amina uses paragraph 2 to begin her essay with a definition of the **key concept** of *economy*. She tells her reader this in the first sentence of the paragraph. However, her definition is also an explanation. On the basis of this **explanation** she makes a **claim**: an increase in employment will have a significant impact on the economy. Finally, she brings in some real **data** or **evidence** on Nike in Vietnam. This links her general explanation of the economy and her general claim about employment to a particular situation – Nike's activity.

In paragraph 3 Amina builds another mini-argument to support her central claim. The next activity explores how she does this.

Activity 3.10

Purpose: to trace the development of the argument in paragraph 3 of Amina's essay.

Task 1: identify the sentences in paragraph 3 which perform the four functions in the table below. They are not necessarily in the same order. Use note-making techniques to reduce these sentences to a few key words and add them to the table.

Introduce the key concept of the paragraph	
Provide data	
Make a claim	
Give an explanation	

Task 2: without looking back at Amina's paragraph, write up your notes from Task 1 as a paragraph. Put the functions in the same order as they are in the table. Pay particular attention to the words you use to link and connect the sentences. Try to use some or all of the words listed below (but use other words if you find them more suitable):

in this process	this is because	the result of this is
this happens because	although	as a result

Compare your answers with those suggested in the Answer section.

Comment

In the previous two activities you practised writing short argument paragraphs. To do this you had to make five decisions:
1   what the paragraph is about – the key concept
2   the sequence for the parts of the argument
3   the way the ideas in the sentences are linked
4   the way the sentences are connected
5   what information will go at the beginning of the sentence and what information will go at the end.

The table below gives an example of each of these decisions. The key concept is in **bold**; the links are <u>underlined</u>; and the connectives are in *italic*.

Argument paragraph		Words chosen
[S1] One of the main influences on an economy is **investment**.	**Concept**	In the first sentence **investment** is the key concept in this paragraph.
[S2] Although <u>Nike does not invest</u> directly, it encourages investment generally by subcontracting production to other companies in the country.	**Data**	Linking information is <u>invest</u>. (*Although* is a connective but it does not connect sentence 2 with sentence 1; it connects the first half of sentence 2 with the second half.)
[S3] *As a result* <u>Nike</u> has a beneficial effect on the economy of developing countries.	**Claim**	Linking information is <u>Nike</u>. The connective is *As a result*.
[S4] <u>This</u> is because investment by Nike leads to new factories being built ...	**Explanation**	Linking information is <u>This</u>. There is no connective.

As the table shows, the key concept of this paragraph says what the paragraph is about: it creates a high-level viewing platform. This is the kind of high-level viewing platform which was missing from the woman's conversation at the bus stop earlier in this session. It gives the reader a frame for the paragraph.

As you saw in the previous two activities, the parts of the argument can be sequenced in different ways. In this activity the sequence is data, claim, explanation. In the previous activity it was claim, data, explanation. It is also possible to use different sequences and to leave out parts.

Links and **connectives** may sound as though they are the same, but in this course they are not. Sentences are linked by the ideas or the information they communicate. The link is usually a kind of repetition of a word or group of words from the first sentence. This is most obvious in the second sentence in the table above. The information that links the two sentences is *investment*. It is easy to see that *Nike does not invest* is linked somehow to the first sentence on *investment*. When two sentences are linked, the link is usually near the beginning of the second sentence.

In the third sentence, the information, *Nike*, is repeated from the second sentence and so this is a link. However, the relationship between these two sentences is also highlighted by the connective *As a result*. These words tell you that this sentence is a result of the previous sentence. Connectives such as this are words which join sentences but do not contain information from the previous sentence. This is why they are called *connectives* and not *links* in this course. *Nike* **is** information from the previous sentence and so it is a link.

Finally, the fourth sentence shows that you don't have to repeat the exact words to link information. *This* is a word that can be used to link to any information. Words like *this* are called **pronouns** because they link to nouns that have gone before. Other words like *this* include *it*, *she*, *he*, *these* and *those*. In this example, *This* links to the whole of the sentence that has gone before.

The fifth decision when you are writing an argument paragraph is what information will go at the beginning of the sentence and at the end of the sentence. Beginnings are important. You have already seen that the beginning paragraph of an essay is important. It tells you what the essay is about. Beginnings of sentences are important for the same reason: they tell you what the sentence is about. Endings are important because they tell you the point of the sentence. The beginning and the ending of sentences work together to tell you **what the sentence is about** and **what the point of the sentence is** as shown below.

What is the sentence about?	What is the point?
Although Nike does not invest directly,	it encourages investment generally by subcontracting production to other companies in the country.
As a result Nike	has a beneficial effect on the economy of developing countries
This	is because investment by Nike leads to new factories being built ...

You have now met the idea that what comes at the beginning – of the essay, of a paragraph or of a sentence – is important. It is important because it tells you what the essay, the paragraph or the sentence is about. You saw this in the bus stop conversation. Because the speaker did not say what she was talking about at the beginning, the listener did not understand her. In this course the information at the beginning is called the theme. If it is the beginning of the essay, it is the **essay theme**: it tells you what the essay is about. If it is the beginning of the paragraph, it is the **paragraph theme**: it tells you what the paragraph is about. If it is the beginning of the sentence, it is the **sentence theme**: it tells you what the sentence is about.

You may often notice that essay themes and paragraph themes contain key concepts. These are usually abstract nouns which are like high-level viewing platforms giving an overview of the text. As you have seen, this paragraph has the key concept, *investment*, in the theme sentence of the paragraph. This paragraph is about *investment*. However, there can also be key concepts in sentences that are not theme sentences. This paragraph has another key concept, *multiplier effect*, which is not in the theme sentence.

Sentence themes are important for a second reason. As you have seen, they contain information that links the sentence to sentences that have gone before. If a reader cannot link each sentence back to the ones before, they will not understand the point of your writing. This was the problem with the bus stop conversation. Once the speaker gives her listener a paragraph theme in an introduction sentence ('I've got so much to do this afternoon'), her listener can link the sentence themes back to this paragraph theme and the conversation makes sense.

Finally, sentence themes must be followed by points. You have just seen how three sentences from paragraph 3 start with a sentence theme and end with the point of the sentence. All these sentence points add up to make a paragraph point; and all the paragraph points add up to make the essay point. By the time your reader has finished your essay, they should be clear what the point of your essay is. By processing the essay title in this way, you create an essay which is about the subject of the title and has a point – or several points. This is the added value of your essay.

The next activity uses the remaining part of the paragraph to reinforce the five features of argument.

Activity 3.11 ....

Purpose: to reinforce the five features of an argument paragraph.

Task: Extract H below is the final sentences from the paragraph in the Answer section for Activity 3.10. You already know the theme of the paragraph – investment is associated with a healthy economy. Now answer the following questions.

1   Which part of the argument is this – **claim**, **evidence** or **explanation**?

2   For each sentence what word or words **link** it to the sentences before? Underline them.

3   Are the word or words you underlined in (2) what the sentence is **about**?

4   What is **the point** of each sentence? Draw a box round it.

5   Are there any **connectives**? Draw a circle round them.

> ### Extract H
>
> This happens because of a process known as the multiplier effect. In this process initial income is used to consume goods and this creates new income; the new income leads to demand for new goods, which in turn leads to demand for labour. The result of this is an increase in employment.

Compare your answers with those suggested in the Answer section.

Comment ....

The success of your essay depends on all the communication and study skills you have practised in Sessions 2 and 3 so far. The secret of your success depends on the design of your argument. You have seen how arguments work on a small scale in two paragraphs of an essay but a successful argument has to work throughout a whole essay. The next activity looks at how Amina manages this.

Activity 3.12 ....

Purpose: to investigate the argument structure of the rest of Amina's essay.

Task: in this set of tasks you will work through the rest of Amina's essay, focusing on the five features of argument structure introduced above.

1   Why could paragraph 4 be seen as a second introductory paragraph to the essay? Does it make a claim? If so, what kind of basis is given for the claim?

2   What is the key concept in the theme sentence of paragraph 5? Paragraph 5 has two claim sentences, two evidence or data

sentences, and one explanation sentence. Identify which sentences are which.

For each sentence, use different coloured pens to box, circle and underline the following:

words that tell you what the sentence is **about**

words that tell you **the point** of the sentence

words that **link** the sentence to sentences before

connectives.

What is the source of the evidence in this paragraph?

3   Paragraph 6 has two key concepts. What are they? The first key concept has an explanation and a claim. Which sentence is which? Which words link sentence 3 to the sentence before it? The second key concept has a Claim but no explanation. Which sentence makes the claim?

4   Paragraph 7 is about a new key concept. What is this concept? Why isn't this key concept introduced in the first sentence of the paragraph? (This is a question about **links**.) Write down the claim and the explanation from this paragraph in your own words.

5   Paragraph 8 has two concluding claims and one explanation. Write down in your own words Amina's concluding claim. Circle a connective in this paragraph.

Compare your answers with those suggested in the Answer section.

Comment   ....

Amina uses concepts and models from her business studies course to build her argument. The concepts are high-level viewing platforms in her text and often (although not always) are in the first sentence of each paragraph. She uses them to explain how and why things happen in the economies of developing countries generally. Then she links this to real world information about Nike and other companies involved in particular developing countries.

In this way, Amina moves up and down between concepts, claims, explanations and evidence. She uses the beginnings of sentences to say what the sentence is about and the ends to make her points. She links and connects sentences so that her reader can follow her argument. Because she is managing all of these features of argument writing, she does not use a single pattern in her paragraphs. Sometimes the claim comes first; sometimes it is one of the other parts of the argument. The key concepts help her reader to see what is going on – they provide an overview and an orientation.

Activity 3.13   ....

Purpose: to practise designing an argument.

Task: in this activity you will work with the ideas from a successful student essay on the same subject as Amina's. As with all essays, there are some differences in the concepts used and in the way the argument is designed. However, you can still judge it using the criteria in the essay-writing checklist in Section 3.2. You will work with the ideas in paragraphs 3 to 6 of the essay.

(a) Paragraph 3

The eight sentences in paragraph 3 below have been mixed up. Reorganise them to make a paragraph that begins with one theme sentence, is followed by six explanation sentences, and ends with a claim sentence. Use links between the sentences to help you decide the order. You may find it helpful to write the sentences out as you organise them.

[S1] The demand by households for goods and services from firms generates interest in this area, encouraging the businesses to invest in improving their services or increase the standard or choice of goods they have to offer. [S2] This increases the flow of income and helps the economy to grow. [S3] To examine how investment might influence the economy we can first look at the 'circular flow of income' model (Coates, 2000, pp. 56–8). [S4] This shows how investment by a company like Nike could help cash flow to circulate through a country's economy by offering jobs and wages to the residents. [S5] There are four economic agents involved in this model: households, firms, banks and the government. [S6] Extra revenue can also be generated through the export of goods to other countries. [S7] Once income has been generated by a household, for example through its residents receiving payment by an employer, this money can be used to purchase goods and to pay taxes and therefore benefit the economy. [S8] In order to invest in this way they are able to take out bank loans or sometimes receive government grants.

(b) Paragraph 4

The following sentence has been removed from paragraph 4 below. Where does it belong in the paragraph? Is it a theme, claim, data / evidence, or an explanation?

> If Nike were to give jobs to the community of a developing country the 'multiplier effect' could be implemented on a grand scale, the level of which would be determined by how many jobs were created and how much the workers received as payment.

[S1] Another example of how investment quickly accumulates and filters through an economy can be shown by the 'multiplier effect' (Coates, 2000, p. 60). [S2] This is where one sum of money can be distributed through society by an initial person investing a part of their total funds in a company, which retains some of what they have obtained and invests the rest in another person, product or service. [S3] The process then continues until the money is exhausted.

(c) Paragraph 5

The table below contains the first sentence of paragraph 5 in full and notes on the remaining sentences. Use the information in the table to write out the paragraph in full. Keep the argument parts in the same order but use as many additional words as you need to say what each sentence is about, what its point is, and to link and connect the sentences.

Theme	Income is not the sole factor that helps to boost an economy, however.
Topic	New and transferable skills and technology for new Nike employees.
Claim	Developing country could utilise in other areas of society.
Claim	Help other businesses with new skills.
Evidence	E.g., Nike factories in less developed countries such as South Korea and Taiwan, 'shoes for different companies are often manufactured simultaneously on neighbouring production lines' ('Keep on running', p. 26).
Explanation	Workers could leave and start up factories with these new skills and technological procedures ☐ more economic growth.

(d) Paragraph 6

In the paragraph below **the links** (the beginning) and **the points** (the end) in the first sentence are in the correct order but the links and the points of all the following sentences have been switched round. Rewrite the paragraph so that the beginning of each sentence links to the sentences before and the rest of the sentence makes a point. You won't need to find new ideas for each sentence but, when you move the parts of the sentences round, you will usually need to use some other words to join the parts together.

I have so far discussed how a business like Nike could influence the economic health of a developing country, but it is possible that its influence on such an economy could be minimal, due to the phenomenon of globalisation. Even poorer countries are able to sustain a stable economy by trading with other, richer countries thanks to global 'deregulation, technological advances and financial management innovations' (Rastogi, 2000, p. 75). 'The opening of the world economies (which) has resulted in more international trade and increased capital among countries' (Rastogi, 2000, p. 78) has come from deregulation. Investment from Nike would not necessarily be required as much as in previous times because international trade results in capital being brought into these countries. Therefore, minimal influence may be felt by the economy.

Compare your answers with those suggested in the Answer section.

Comment ....

In this activity you focused on how the **sentences** work together in the design of an argument paragraph. In a whole essay, the **paragraphs** have to work together in a similar way to build the argument. The same questions arise in designing an essay as in designing a paragraph, as follows.

- Theme: What is this paragraph about?
- Point: What is the point of the paragraph?
- Links: How does it link to the other paragraphs?
- Connectives: How is it connected?
- Argument structure: Is it a claim and/or evidence and/or explanation?

As mentioned earlier, when you build an argument throughout the whole essay like this, the introduction is a high-level viewing platform which allows you and your reader to see clearly across the whole argument. This is why the central claim in the introduction is so powerful. Once you have moved out of the introduction, your reader needs to be kept focused on your argument. The opening sentences of each paragraph are good places to do this. They say what the paragraph is about. They should also link directly back to the introduction or to one of the previous paragraphs. There are also connectives which can be used to connect paragraphs, just as there are connectives that connect sentences. Finally, paragraphs must have a point. If your reader comes to the end of a paragraph which has not got a point they will read on anyway. However, if that happens a few times they will begin to lose the will to read on. This is why it is important to plan your essay with a point-based outline rather than a concept-based outline (see Session 2). A concept-based outline is what your essay is **about**. A point-based outline is **what you want to say about it**, i.e. the points you want to make.

To bring together all the ideas that have been introduced in this session so far, in the next activity you will use the criteria sheet to evaluate an essay. This activity will help you to practise evaluating an argument structure. After this final look at an example essay, you will return to the draft essay you wrote in Session 2 and revise it in the light of the input from this session. Finally, you will send your own essay to two members of your tutor group for evaluation and use the evaluation sheet yourself to evaluate two essays from your tutor group.

Activity 3.14 ....

Purpose: to practise evaluating an argument essay.
Task: using the checklist of criteria in Box 3.1 (p.71), evaluate Text 3.2 in Resource Book 2. Write up your evaluation – either as a table or as a report.

At this point a few words are necessary about two aspects of argument writing which have not been covered in this session: the use of source material and essay conclusions. Source material was the focus of Session 2 and, because the focus of Session 3 is on argument structure, source material has only been mentioned in passing but it is central to argument. Case studies and other primary source material provide the data or evidence from the real world of business. Business course texts – that is, secondary source material – provide the concepts and models that you use for the explanation and so they are also part of the basis for your claims. Business course texts can also provide data or evidence. This is because they are written by 'authorities', as discussed in Session 2. This is one reason for making clear in your essay where your explanation has come from. If you provide a reference for an explanation in your essay, it is a kind of evidence that the explanation is valid.

Many arguments are not based on any primary source material at all. In academic business studies arguments can be developed just by comparing explanations from different authorities and providing references as the evidence. There is more on this use of source material in argument in Session 4.

Finally, the checklist refers to the **conclusion** of an essay. So far, you have not examined any conclusions. They are dealt with more thoroughly in Session 4. Some students find the conclusion the most difficult part of an essay to write. In this session, you might like to use your existing knowledge of conclusions in making your evaluations. The most important thing to say about a conclusion is that it should make clear what the point of an essay is.

Activity 3.15   ....

Purpose: to implement the principles of argument writing introduced in this session.

Task: using the following procedure, write a final draft of the essay you began in Session 2, '*Discuss the extent to which a large corporation such as Nike might influence the economic health of a developing country*'.

1   Review the outline or the first draft you wrote in Session 2. Use the list of criteria in part B of the essay-writing checklist in Section 3.2. Does your outline or draft make any claims? Do you explain your claims? Have you included any evidence for your claims? Use any further information you have learned while studying the essays in this session to improve your outline or draft. Remember the rules of plagiarism and use the information without copying it.

2   Rewrite your first draft. Pay attention to all the features of argument structure which are in the checklist and which you have practised. In particular pay attention to the essay introduction. Does it say what the essay is about? Does it make a central claim? For each paragraph, does the beginning sentence say what topic the paragraph is about? Do you have claims, evidence and explanations? Do your sentences begin by saying what they are about and do they end by making points? Are the sentences linked by their information and connected by connecting words?

3   Use the checklist to check all these features.

3.4 Critical reflection

In this session you have seen how, although there are some common features to the design of an argument essay, students also respond to essay titles in different ways. In your Learning Journal reflect on your views on the design of an essay. Focus on the following questions.

1   As you wrote the final draft of the essay in Activity 3.15, did you use any of the ideas about essay design which were introduced in this session? How?

2   Do you agree that it is possible to speak about 'the design' of an essay? Why?

3   Do you think there are likely to be similarities in the design of different students' essays? Why?

4   Do you think it is important for students to try to be original when they write an essay? Why?

Use the online Learning Journal for your personal reflection.

3.5 Review

In this session you have:

- examined some essay texts to see how the argument structure is developed, using key concepts, claims, evidence or data and explanations

- observed how introductions to essays, paragraphs and sentences say what they are about, i.e. they give the theme; how essays, paragraphs and sentences make points; how information is used to link sentences and paragraphs; and how connectives are used to connect sentences and paragraphs

- practised using some of these features to write an essay

- developed your knowledge of the criteria used to evaluate argument essays.

3.6 Answer section

Activity 3.2

The introduction ends with the first paragraph.

The conclusion is probably the last two paragraphs. You might say that it is only the last paragraph but this is a rather general paragraph that does not really deal with the argument which is introduced in the first paragraph. Paragraph 8 does this best.

The paragraphs give a clue. The introduction will be at least the first paragraph and the conclusion will be the last one; but there is sometimes more than one paragraph in an introduction or a conclusion.

There are several other reasons why paragraph 1 is the introduction and paragraphs 8 and 9 are the conclusion. These are explored further in this session.

Activity 3.3

Statement	In Amina's introduction	Not in Amina's introduction	Words in introduction
1		✓	the scale of its activity will have an effect on the locality
2		✓	in a developing country ... significant influence on the whole economy
3	✓		a clear link
4		✓	Ibegins with investment then goes on to consider four indicators
5	✓		although ... is beneficial, there are some negative impacts

Activity 3.4

Function	Which words do these jobs?
Link back to the title	Many references to influence, effect, economy, Nike, economic health, large corporations
Give a general background to the topic	S1 and S2
Identify the key concepts in the essay	Economy, investment, indicators of economic health, beneficial and negative impacts
State the essay's central argument	S4
Say how the essay will be organised	S5

Activity 3.5

Extract B This paper argues that the extent to which MNCs influence the economic health of a developing country is dependent on that country's response to the corporation.

Extract C <u>Arguably, large corporations support development and economic growth in developing countries, but is there evidence that corporate growth and corporate malpractice can produce disadvantage?</u>

Neither claim is exactly the same as Amina's but Extract B is probably the closest since it focuses on the fact there are positive **and** negative impacts of investment by MNCs.

Activity 3.6

Extract D: sentence (d); after sentence 2. Function = central claim

Extract E: sentence (c); after sentence 8. Function = how essay will be organised

Extract F: sentence (a); after sentence 1. Function = identifies some key concepts

Extract G: sentence (b); before sentence 1. Function = link to title

Activity 3.7

Concepts: developing country; investment; economy; firms; households; banks; governments; multiplier effect; economic health, stability of employment, living standards, price stability, the balance of payments.

Model: circular flow of income.

Activity 3.9

Task 1

(a) The economy: a system for the exchange of resources; (b) firms; (c) households.

Task 2

Labour (work is created for a large number of people); because a multinational corporation starts up in the country; there will be a change in the exchange of resources: more people will be employed and more goods will be bought.

Task 3

Data	Nike is Vietnam's biggest employer.
Claim	*This means that* ... Nike will have a significant impact on the exchange of resources.
Explanation	*Because* ... the economy is a system for the exchange of resources in which the main economic agents are households and firms. A big employer will need a large number of employees and will create employment for households.

Task 4

Claim	Nike will have a significant impact on the exchange of resources in Vietnam
Data	*since* it is Vietnam's biggest employer
Explanation	*This is because* the economy is a system for the exchange of resources. A big employer will need a large number of employees and will create employment for households.

Task 5

The sequence is: explanation (an economy is a system for the exchange ...); claim (if work is created ...); data (Nike is Vietnam's biggest employer).

Activity 3.10

Task 1

Topic	Investment
Data	Nike does not invest directly but encourages investment by subcontracting production
Claim	Nike has beneficial influence
Explanation	Factories built → money injected → more econ possibilities (← multiplier effect: initial income → consuming goods → new income → demand for goods → demand for labour → more employment)

Task 2

Here is an example which uses all the connecting words. Yours will be different.

One of the main influences on an economy is investment. *Although* Nike does not invest directly, it encourages investment generally by subcontracting production to other companies in the country. *As a result* Nike has a beneficial effect on the economy of developing countries. *This is because* investment by Nike leads to new factories being built, more money being injected into the economy and the creation of more economic possibilities. *This happens because* of a process known as the multiplier effect. *In this process* initial income is used to consume goods and this creates new income; the new income leads to demand for new goods, which in turn leads to demand for labour. *The result of this is* an increase in employment.

Activity 3.11

1   Explanation.
2   This; In this process; The result of this.
3   Yes.
4   The point of each sentence is all the remaining information in each sentence.
5   *The result of this* is a combined connective (*the result*) and link (*this*).

Activity 3.12

1   Paragraph 4 introduces four new key concepts which organise the next three paragraphs. The claim is that the picture of economic health is more complicated. The basis for the claim is the reference to the business studies author, Coates.

2   The key concept is stability of employment. S1 and S5 are claim sentences; S2 and S3 are evidence or data sentences; S4 is an explanation sentence.

In the following version of paragraph 5 **bold words** are what the sentence is **about**; underlined words are **the point** of the sentence; *italicised words* are **the links**; and [words in brackets] are the connectives.

Stability of employment is not really a factor that companies like Nike are offering directly to the *developing economies* in which they operate. **When costs increased in *South Korea and Taiwan*, for example**, training shoe manufacturing was moved to lower cost locations such as Indonesia, Thailand and China (Sturges, 2000, p. 27). **The benefit to the *economies of Taiwan and Korea*** was not entirely lost, however, because 'the trend has been to continue to use *the same Korean and Taiwanese manufacturers*, who have set up and managed production plants in the new geographic locations' (Sturges, 2000, p. 27). **The money brought into the economy by *these firms*** should create *employment* indirectly. **[Therefore], although *Nike* does not offer stability of *employment levels* directly**, its use of local companies as subcontractors is helping to create profits, which, if reinvested, can help employment levels.

The source of evidence is the case study by Sturges.

3   Two key concepts are rising living standards and the ability to control inflation.
    The first key concept, S1, is the explanation; S2 is the claim.
    Words that link S3 to the sentence before it: control inflation, keep prices stable.
    The second key concept is in S4; a claim.

4   The new concept is balance of payments.
    This is not introduced in the first sentence because S1 of paragraph 7 makes a link back to *increased demand* in paragraph 6. S1 then makes the point that this leads to *imported goods*. *Imported goods* is then used as the theme of S2 so it makes a link to S1. Then S2 makes a point about *imported goods* which is *balance of payments*.
    The first explanation is that a country which imports goods without exporting will have a balance of payments problem. The claim is that developing countries have a disadvantage with this. Then there is a further explanation: they don't have financial skills or capital to compete with the West.

5   Multinational companies have a great impact on economies where they operate but in a developing economy this will not necessarily benefit the country.
    The connective is *however*.

Activity 3.13

All of the original paragraphs can be seen in Resource Book 2, Text 3.2.

Paragraph 3

1 (S3), 2 (S5), 3 (S7), 4 (S1), 5 (S8), 6 (S2), 7 (S6), 8 (S4).

Paragraph 4

The missing sentence goes after sentence 3. It is mainly a claim but with an explanation in the second half of the sentence.

Paragraph 5

See Text 3.2 in Resource Book 2 for the original paragraph.

Paragraph 6

See Text 3.2 in Resource Book 2 for the original paragraph.

SESSION 4 **Writing a critical discussion**

4.1 Introduction

By now you should realise that it is helpful to think of essay writing as a series of stages, or processes, which you work through in order to produce a completed text – a successful product. Session 2 highlighted the importance of having a clear understanding of an essay title and you learned that it was essential to understand exactly what you are being asked to do. In particular, the significance of instruction words and key concepts in a title was emphasised. In Sessions 1 and 3 you also considered the meaning of 'argument' in an essay. In Session 1 you learned how argument in writing does not necessarily involve two contrasting ideas or views but may more usefully be thought of as a 'thread of meaning' which is developed during the essay. Session 3 developed further the idea of argument as a claim supported by evidence and explanation. In this session, the idea of argument is developed even further by looking at what it means to be 'critical' in your writing.

In Session 3, you focused on an essay as a finished product. By looking at examples of student essays, you considered how the writers integrated the three elements of an essay: the introduction, the body and the conclusion. Session 4 will also focus on the product at the end of the writing process. However, the main focus of this session is to consider how writers can develop a critical aspect to their work. You will consider what being critical in writing means and look at ways in which you can incorporate a critical aspect into your writing. To do this, you will consider a specific essay title. You will evaluate examples of how students responded to this title by again using the essay-writing checklist from Session 2. You will refer back to the two sections of this checklist that you have already worked with – Section A 'Use of source materials' and Section B 'Structure of an essay' – and you will begin to work with the third section – Section C 'Academic writing style'.

Learning outcomes

In this session, you will:

- consider the requirements for a specific essay on markets by careful analysis of its title
- develop your understanding of the topic of this essay by analysing the work of other students
- consider aspects of paraphrasing and the use of business studies language
- develop an approach to reading texts critically, focusing on the importance of the language of argument
- explore the idea of critical discussion in writing
- critically review samples of student essays based on the essay title and evaluate how students' viewpoints are represented in their work
- review features of essay introductions and conclusions.

4.2 Understanding what is required

In Session 2 you practised analysing an essay title in order to determine what was required. To do this you identified the instruction words and the key concepts. The first activity in this session introduces the essay title which you will consider in some detail in this session.

Activity 4.1 ....

Purpose: to review the practice of analysing an essay title.

Task: analyse the essay title that will be considered in this session:

Critically discuss why markets may fail to deliver socially desirable outcomes.

Make notes about the title in the table below. Use the following questions to help you.

- What are the instruction words? How are these instruction words significant for writing this essay?
- What are the key concepts in the title? Write some questions you could ask in order to learn more about these concepts.

Component	Notes
Instruction words	
Key concepts	

Compare your answers with those suggested in the Answer section.

Comment ....

Your understanding of these instruction words and concepts is important for getting you started on reading source texts. The word *critically* is of central importance to this title as it refers to the way in which the title is discussed. Perhaps a good way to begin is by thinking about the verb for this word: *to criticise*. This word is commonly associated with something negative, such as complaining to the manager of a shop about the poor service you received.

However, in the context of writing an academic text, critical discussion is positive. It means to evaluate ideas: that is, **to judge the strengths and weaknesses of a particular explanation, theory or idea, using a considered argument to support your points**. This definition can give some guidance for how to approach an answer to this essay title. Once again, you can see the appearance of the idea of argument but, importantly, there is also the idea of evaluating something, such as the strengths and weaknesses of other people's arguments.

Critical discussion is a good example of an academic style of writing. For this reason, here you will begin to work with Section C of the essay-writing checklist: 'Control of academic writing style'. Section C focuses on the kind of language used in business studies texts.

4.3 Understanding the topic

This section involves a series of activities that will help you to understand better the topic represented in the essay title. To do this, first you will look at some key concepts business tutors consider relevant to this essay, including:

- the market
- the meaning of market failure
- various kinds of market failure
- externalities
- government intervention
- public goods
- ignorance and uncertainty.

To learn more about these concepts, you will look at the source texts students use for this essay. You will also have the opportunity to focus on particular language used in these texts as well as to develop your skills in critical reading and paraphrasing.

The market

Activity 4.2 ....

Purpose: to introduce the concept of the market.

Task 1: you will work with Text 4.1 in Resource Book 2. Before you read it, look at the following questions.

(a) From the heading, what do you expect the text to be about?

(b) What does paragraph 2 give you?

(c) What example does the writer give to illustrate markets and prices?

(d) What controls the movements of resources in a market?

Task 2: now read Text 4.1, looking for answers to the questions above.

Task 3: after you have read it once, read the text again and answer the following questions.

(a) What example is given of buyers and sellers physically meeting?

(b) What kind of market is the stock market?

(c) Prices control the market activity of which economic factors?

(d) Why is a steak consumed by 'someone else'?

(e) What markets are involved in buying a hamburger?

Compare your answers with those suggested in the Answer section.

Comment

The market is the key concept in the essay title you are looking at in this session. The description in Text 4.1 is very general. It says how the markets should work. It does not refer to problems in markets. But, of course, there are problems. As economists say, 'Markets are not perfect'. Like many business studies assignments, students are asked to discuss the problems in their essay. The next activity introduces some of the problems in the markets.

Externalities and socially desirable outcomes

Activity 4.3

Purpose: To develop an understanding of the nature of **externalities** and how they affect **socially desirable outcomes**.

Task: read Text 4.2 in Resource Book 2 and then complete the table below. You should use the active reading strategies you have been practising in this course. However, you don't need to understand the whole text; instead, focus on completing the table below.

Externalities

Cause	Effects	Activity	Examples
Market activities	_____ (negative: socially _____)	Production _____	_____ _____
	_____ (positive: socially _____)	_____	Allowing other firms to access research data
		_____	_____

Compare your answers with those suggested in the Answer section.

Comment

The table above explains how social efficiency cannot be achieved in the market when those who produce and consume goods affect other people when they produce or consume. *External costs* refers to the negative effects of production and consumption, while *external benefits* refers to positive effects of production and consumption. As the text points out, *negative social costs* are the total cost to society of a firm's actions in the production of goods, which includes the *private cost of production* plus any *negative externalities*. Similarly, *social benefits* are the total benefit of a firm's actions and include *private benefits for consumers* plus any *positive externalities*.

The activity above emphasises the important role of *externalities* in preventing desirable social outcomes from the activities of firms. Other important factors that result in markets failing to achieve social efficiency include lack of competition between firms, and the time it takes for markets to adjust to new market conditions.

Government intervention

The problems created by externalities are problems in a *free market*. However, markets are not necessarily free: the government can play a role in influencing marketing conditions. The role of the government in regulating markets is one of the main economic and political questions in many economies.

In the next activity you will think about how the government can influence the effect of externalities for the benefit of society as a whole.

Activity 4.4

Purpose: to understand the role the government can play in helping to deliver desirable social outcomes.

Task 1: the following extracts refer **either** to problems associated with free markets **or** to solutions the government can apply to these problems. Read the extracts and complete the table below by indicating which paragraphs (A–H) refer to problems and which paragraphs refer to solutions.

Extracts

   A   There are several policy instruments that the government can use. At one extreme, it can totally replace the market by providing goods and services itself. At the other extreme, it can merely seek to persuade producers, consumers or workers to act differently. Between the two extremes the government has a number of weapons it can use to change the way markets operate: weapons such as taxes, subsidies, laws and regulatory bodies.

B Thus if the government wants to discourage smoking and drinking, it can put taxes on tobacco and alcohol. In more extreme cases it could make various activities illegal: activities such as prostitution, certain types of gambling, and the sale and consumption of drugs.

C When there are imperfections in the market, social efficiency will not be achieved. Marginal social benefit (MSB) will not equal marginal social cost (MSC). A different level of output would be more desirable.

D The government could either provide them free or subsidise their production.

E Faced with all the problems of the free market, what is a government to do?

F The government may feel that people need protecting from poor economic decisions that they make on their own behalf. It may feel that in a free market people will consume too many harmful things.

G Taxes and subsidies can be used to correct these imperfections. Essentially the approach is to tax those goods or activities where the market produces too much, and subsidise those where the market produces too little.

H On the other hand, the government may feel that people consume too little of things that are good for them: things such as education, health care and sports facilities. When the government feels that it knows better than individuals about what items are good for them, such goods are known as merit goods.

(Sloman and Sutcliffe, 2001)

Problems	Solutions
Paragraphs:	Paragraphs:

Task 2: government involvement in the problems and solutions outlined above can be placed under three headings:
- **protecting people's interests**
- **government intervention in the market**
- **taxes and subsidies**.

In the table below, identify which of paragraphs A–H deal with the problems and solutions for each heading. The first pair has been done as an example.

Heading	Problem	Solution
Protecting people's interests	1 F 2	1 B 2
Government intervention in the market		
Taxes and subsidies		

Compare your answers with those suggested in the Answer section.

Comment

Activities 4.3 and 4.4 highlight two important elements in a discussion of how markets may fail to deliver socially desirable outcomes. You have seen how negative externalities can have a direct effect on social efficiency. You have also seen how governments can have a measure of control over many of these elements and so influence the extent of undesirable social outcomes from firms' activities. Thus for your essay title, you may say that, although governments do not directly address the question of why markets may fail to deliver socially desirable outcomes, a discussion of the role a government plays may be viewed as an important factor in the overall discussion of the topic.

4.4 Academic writing style and paraphrasing

Session 2 focused on a range of ways of using source material to prepare your essay. In Session 3 you looked at some of the ways students used business studies course texts as the basis of the argument in their essay. From these course texts, students learned concepts that they used to explain the ways in which a multinational company affected the economy of a developing country. When you use source material in your essay, you have to make many decisions about how you will adapt it for use in your argument.

One way of using source material is to **paraphrase** it. In simple terms, this means saying the same thing in different words. When you paraphrase academic writing you have to decide how much of the original wording to use. As you saw in Session 1, academic writing often has a particular style – specialised, impersonal, and objective. At the same time, students are often told 'you should write in your own words'.

Trying to write 'in your own words' and also use an academic style can lead to two quite different problems. A student either copies the academic style of the source material too closely and is criticised for **plagiarism** (this is discussed below) or they use everyday language and are criticised for being too conversational in their writing.

In this section, you will do a paraphrasing activity and use the section of the essay-writing checklist dealing with academic style.

In Activity 4.1, one of the key concepts you noted in the essay title was *social responsibility*. Before you read a source text which looks at firms and social responsibility, think about your understanding of what it means to be socially responsible. Perhaps you can think of examples of socially responsible behaviour. Are there any ways in which firms can behave in socially responsible ways? How important is it for them to behave in this way? Thinking about an issue like this before you read a source text helps prepare you for what you will read and helps your understanding.

The following source text on the issue of the social responsibility of firms is taken from Sloman and Sutcliffe (1998, p. 165). In this publication, the authors define *social responsibility* as: 'Where a firm takes into account the interests and concerns of a community rather than just its shareholders.'

Firms and social responsibility

Activity 4.5 ....

Purpose

(a) To focus on paraphrasing skills by using alternative language to the original text.

(b) To focus on academic style in writing and the business studies language for this topic.

Task: Extract A below is adapted from part of Text 4.3 in Resource Book 2. Some words from the original text have been changed (*see italics*). Extract B is the original text but several words have been omitted. These words are listed above the text. They are the original words which have been changed in Extract A. Replace the original words from the list in the correct spaces in Extract B.

Extract A

Firms and social responsibility

It is often assumed that firms are simply concerned to *make as much money as possible*: that they are not concerned with *more general considerations* of social responsibility. What this assumption means is that firms are only concerned with the interests of shareholders (or managers) and are not concerned for the well-being of the *community as a whole.*

It is then argued, however, that *competition* could result in society benefiting from the self-interested behaviour of firms: i.e. that profit maximization will *result in* social efficiency under conditions of perfect competition and the absence of externalities. But, as we have seen, in the real world, markets are not perfect and there are often considerable externalities. In such cases, not enough social responsibility on the part of firms can have *extremely negative* effects on society. Indeed, many forms of market failure can be *explained by* business practices that could not be classified as 'socially responsible': advertising campaigns that *are not honest* or in some way deceive the consumer; monopoly producers *taking advantage of* their monopoly position through charging excessively high prices; the conscious decision to ignore water and air pollution limits, knowing that the chances of being caught are *very low.*

(Adapted from Sloman and Sutcliffe, 1998)

Now replace the following original words and word groups in the spaces in Extract B.

| attribute directly to | broader issues | competitive forces | exploiting | a lack of | seek to misinform |
| maximize profits | lead to | slim | profoundly adverse | at large | |

Extract B

It is often assumed that firms are simply concerned to _____ : that they are not concerned with _____ of social responsibility. What this assumption means is that firms are only concerned with the interests of shareholders (or managers) and are not concerned for the well-being of the community _____ .

It is then argued, however, that _____ could result in society benefiting from the self-interested behavior of firms: i.e. that profit maximization will _____ social efficiency under conditions of perfect competition and the absence of externalities. But, as we have seen, in the real world, markets are not perfect and there are often considerable externalities. In such cases, _____ social responsibility on the part of firms can have _____ effects on society. Indeed, many forms of market failure can be _____ business practices that could not be classified as 'socially responsible': advertising campaigns that _____ or in some way deceive the consumer;

> monopoly producers _____ their monopoly position through charging excessively high prices; the conscious decision to ignore water and air pollution limits, knowing that the chances of being caught are _____ .
>
> (Adapted from Sloman and Sutcliffe, 1998)

Compare your answers with those suggested in the Answer section.

Comment

This activity demonstrates how paraphrasing a text involves thinking about the alternative language you can use to express the same information. Here, you did not, of course, paraphrase each sentence completely. You simply began this process by thinking of other words and phrases you could use instead of some of those in the original text. Full paraphrasing generally involves changing the grammar of the sentence as well as the vocabulary. The extent to which you can do this will affect the quality of your writing. This means you should do this task carefully in order to avoid writing a text which is too close to the original. A text that is too close to an original text is **plagiarised**. It is also important that you reference the source text correctly or this will also be seen as plagiarism.

In the essay-writing checklist, plagiarism is included in Section A 'Use of source material'. This section was introduced in Session 2, although plagiarism was not covered there. When a student plagiarises a source text by copying it out, a tutor will get the impression that the student doesn't really understand the ideas they are writing about. This is why tutors expect students to use their own words when they write essays.

However, this is not as easy as it sounds. One reason is that in saying 'use your own words', tutors do not expect students to use any words they like. For example, they do not expect students to use words in the same way that they would use them in a conversation. You studied some of the differences between conversation and academic writing in Session 1.

When tutors ask students to use their own words, they mean their 'own academic words'. For this reason, paraphrase and plagiarism are also relevant to Section C of the essay-writing checklist, 'Academic writing style'. This section is introduced after two more activities on paraphrasing. The business studies concepts relevant to the markets assignment in these activities are *ignorance* and *uncertainty*.

Ignorance and uncertainty

Activity 4.6

Purpose: to examine the strengths and weaknesses of a student's paraphrase of source text.

Task: read Text 4.4 in Resource Book 2, which is a business studies course text on the role of *ignorance and uncertainty* in market failure. Then read Text 4.5, which is an extract from Robin's essay on markets and social responsibility. Think about the strengths and weaknesses of Robin's paraphrase by comparing the two texts. Then return here and write comments in the right-hand column below next to each of Robin's sentences. Focus on the quality of Robin's paraphrasing compared with the original text. The first one is done for you as an example.

Robin's paragraph	Comments
1 Lack of information and uncertainty can also lead to market failure.	1 This opening sentence clearly identifies the theme of this paragraph.
2 Perfect competition assumes that consumers, firms and factor suppliers have perfect knowledge of costs and benefits – often this is not the case.	2
3 Consumers may only purchase some products or services once and therefore have no previous experience on which to base their decision, exacerbated by advertising messages and persuasive sales techniques.	3
4 Similarly, firms are often ignorant of market opportunities, prices, costs, rival activity, productivity of factors, etc.	4
5 Consumer and organisational decisions made in the absence of sufficient information can often be wrong and result in market failure. (Source: Suneja (2000) *Understanding Business: Markets*)	5

Compare your answers with those suggested in the Answer section.

Comment

Although the paragraph begins with a clear theme sentence, it contains inconsistent paraphrasing which reduces the quality of this work. Robin does refer to the original source of the information at the end of the paragraph, but this is not really enough. In several places, Robin copies sentences which each require quotation marks and source references but it is not appropriate to have so much quotation. In this situation, paraphrasing is the best solution.

Activity 4.7

Purpose: to examine examples of the changes students made when paraphrasing a source text.

Task: compare the source text in Extracts C and F below (from Text 4.4 in Resource Book 2) with the student paraphrases in Extracts D, E and G. What language did the students use to paraphrase the source text? Write it in the table below the extracts.

Extract C (source text)

> Consumers may not be aware of the quality of such goods until they have purchased them, by which time it is too late. Advertising may contribute to people's ignorance by misleading them as to the benefits of a good.
>
> (Sloman and Sutcliffe, 2001)

Extract D (Julie's paraphrase)

In fact, firms are possibly unaware of market opportunities. Consumers might have little information, or information through advertising might be misleading ...

Extract E (Tom's paraphrase)

However, in reality, individuals and organisations may not have the information to be able to equate these costs and benefits (Sloman & Sutcliffe, 1998, p. 150). For example, individuals could be misled by peers into thinking a premium brand of washing powder is more effective than a bargain brand ...

Extract C	Julie	Tom
... may not be aware of ...		
Advertising may contribute to people's ignorance by misleading them ...		

Extract F (source text)

Many economic decisions are based on expected future conditions. Since the future can never be known for certain, many decisions will be taken that in retrospect will be seen to have been wrong.

(Sloman and Sutcliffe, 2001)

Extract G (Guy's paraphrase)

Many business decisions are also made in expectation of future circumstances, and the full information will never be available before the decision. There is an inevitable element of risk as to the outcome of such decisions.

Extract F (source text)	Guy
economic	
expected future conditions	
many decisions will be taken that in retrospect will be seen to have been wrong.	

Compare your answers with those suggested in the Answer section.

Comment

These extracts show some of the changes the students made when they paraphrased information from the source material. These changes ranged from individual words, to word groups, up to whole sentences. The paraphrased language may have exactly the same meaning as the original language, or only approximately the same meaning (for example, *economic* and *business* in Guy's paraphrase). This may or may not be important in a given text but, in some cases, it may be significant. Deciding whether a word should be paraphrased or not, and then deciding whether a paraphrase means the same as the original text is part of having critical awareness.

Sometimes it is not appropriate to paraphrase a business studies word (for example, *the market*) or word group (for example, *social responsibility*). Often these are words for the key concepts you are studying in the business studies course. They are the technical terms of business studies and you are expected to use them. However, there are many words which are used by the writers of business studies texts which you do need to paraphrase. Sometimes these words may also seem technical but they are part of the general academic style of these texts. If you do not paraphrase them, you will be plagiarising. However, when writing them in your own words, you are still expected to use an academic writing style. In this way, you develop your own academic writing style. Section C of the essay-writing checklist deals with this kind of writing style, as follows.

Box 4.1   Checklist for a successful essay

C Control of academic writing style – does the writing style conform to appropriate patterns of written academic English?

1   Appropriate choice of vocabulary
2   Appropriate use of business concept words
3   Appropriate use of other abstract words
4   Appropriate combinations of words
5   Appropriate relationship with reader
6   Appropriate evaluation language

Source: adapted from materials created by Helen Bonano and Janet Jones, MASUS Project, University of Sydney, 1997.

Looking at these criteria more closely: C1 is a general criterion and means using the kind of words which are generally suitable for an academic essay. Session 1 of this book gave you some ideas about what these are like. Criterion C2 refers to the language of technical business studies mentioned above. For example, the source Text 4.3 gives an overview of the relationship between *firms* and *social responsibility*. The authors refer to how *social efficiency* can result from *perfect competition*, but that this is not possible because of *externalities*. All of these business terms are relevant to this essay title. The concept of *externalities* is particularly important in understanding a central theme in the essay title; that is, 'why markets may fail to deliver socially desirable outcomes.' To write a successful essay on this theme, you need to use these business concept words.

However, these business concept words are from academic business studies texts in which business studies specialists use such terms in combination with other abstract and academic words. This is what criteria C1–C4 cover. Together, all these words – the business concepts and the general academic words – make the style of professional communication for business studies. As a student of business studies, you will learn this style as you work with business studies texts and ideas; but, to some extent, you will also develop a style of your own.

So, criteria C1–C4 refer to the way you use the language of business studies without plagiarising. These criteria combine partly with the criteria in Section B, which deal with the structure of your argument, and Section A, which deal with using source material.

Finally, there are criteria C5 and C6: using the language of critical evaluation. As you develop your own style of professional communication, using the language of business studies, you will also develop the language of critical evaluation. Critical evaluation was introduced at the beginning of this session and is considered further in the next section.

4.5 Establishing a critical argument

The comment in Activity 4.1 defines the idea of critical discussion in an essay title as follows: **to judge the strengths and weaknesses of a particular topic, theory or idea, using carefully considered argument to support your points**. This definition was described as central to how you should approach writing this kind of essay. The comment also referred to the idea of judging such factors as the strengths and weaknesses of other people's arguments. The activities in this section consider what this means in terms of how you read a source text. This is important because, if you are going to critically discuss something in your writing, you must first be able to critically analyse the texts you read.

In Session 3, you studied how students built arguments in their essays. The arguments are made up of three parts: **claims**, **explanation**, and **data** or **evidence**. In these essays, the writers generally agreed with the explanations they gave. They did not question whether these explanations were correct. Similarly, they generally accepted the data or evidence they used. They did not question whether this data was accurate. So generally, the essay pattern was a claim, based on data or evidence, and an explanation.

One way to establish a critical argument is to question these parts. You can question the claim, the data or the explanation – and often all three. The next activity introduces this kind of critical argument.

Activity 4.8 ....

Purpose: to develop a critical understanding of building an argument in a text.

Task 1: read Text 4.3 in Resource Book 2 and then return to this activity.

Task 2: in the left-hand column below there are six sentences from Text 4.3. In the right-hand column there is a description of each sentence but they are in the wrong order. Match the sentences on the left with the correct descriptions on the right by identifying the correct description.

Paragraph sentence	Description of sentence
1 It is often assumed that firms are simply concerned to maximize profits: that they are not concerned with broader issues of social responsibility. (**Description**: _____)	(a) Presents contradictory real world data in order to question the initial **claims**.
2 What this assumption means is that firms are only concerned with the interests of shareholders (or managers) and are not concerned for the well-being of the community at large. (**Description**: _____)	(b) Expands a **claim** or an assumption by giving more detail.
3 It is then argued, however, that competitive forces could result in society benefiting from the self-interested behaviour of firms: i.e. that profit maximization will lead to social efficiency under conditions of perfect competition and the absence of externalities. (**Description**: _____)	(c) Provides **basis** for new **claim** by giving evidence of specific examples from real world.
4 But, as we have seen, in the real world, markets are not perfect and there are often considerable externalities. (**Description**: _____)	(d) Presents a **claim** or an assumption, i.e. what many people accept as being the truth about firms.
5 In such cases, a lack of social responsibility on the part of firms can have profoundly adverse effects on society. (**Description**: _____)	(e) Presents a second related **claim** and **explains** the logic of that claim.
6 Indeed, many forms of market failure can be attributed directly to business practices that could not be classified as 'socially responsible': advertising campaigns that seek to misinform or in some way deceive the consumer; monopoly producers exploiting their monopoly position through charging excessively high prices; the conscious decision to ignore water and air pollution limits; knowing that the chances of being caught are slim. (**Description**: _____)	(f) Makes a new and contradictory **claim**.

There are no suggested answers for this activity.

Comment

There are no suggested answers for this activity because it aims to prompt you to reflect a little more on the parts of an argument. Sometimes it can be difficult to identify what is a **claim**, an **explanation**, **evidence** or **data**. For this reason, it is not always useful to worry about whether to call some information a claim, an explanation or data. Sometimes an explanation is also data at the same time. Sometimes an explanation can also be a new claim. The important point is not to be correct about which is which but to think about how arguments are made up of parts. It is not enough just to make claims. Claims need a basis – some kind of explanation or evidence. Also, it is not enough to question a claim. Your question needs some kind of basis – a different explanation or different data.

In this case, you should note first that, as a critical reader, Text 4.3 presents more than one side to the argument about firms and social responsibility. However, you should also note that more than one side to the argument does not lead to confusion in the writing. The text develops towards a single conclusion: that is, how firms are **not** socially responsible. Note how this is done: partly by the way the writer organises the parts of the argument; partly by argument language which makes clear how the argument is structured; partly by links and connectives (introduced in Session 3). In these ways, the writer makes it clear how each point in the argument builds on the previous points.

The language a writer uses to build the argument is referred to in criteria C5 and C6 of the essay-writing checklist. This is the language of evaluation (criterion C6). However, as you may remember from Session 1, how you express an evaluation is part of a writer's relationship with their reader. The way a writer of an academic text expresses opinions and judgements is different from the way a company expresses opinions and judgements in its company website or the way a sportsperson expresses their evaluation of a new training shoe.

Activities 4.9 to 4.11 look at some of the language for building an argument. You may notice that there is an overlap with Section B of the checklist, 'Structure and development of the text'. The language and structure of academic text are naturally connected.

Activity 4.9

Purpose: to identify the argument language, links and connectives in the development of an argument.

Task: look again at Text 4.3 in Resource Book 2, and answer the questions below about the text features used to develop the argument.

1   *It is often assumed that firms are simply concerned to maximize profits: that they are not concerned with broader issues of social responsibility.*
    What is your understanding of the expression *It is often assumed* here?

    _____

    _____

    _____

2   *What this assumption means is that firms are only concerned with the interests of shareholders (or managers) and are not concerned for the well-being of the community at large.*
    What does *this assumption* refer to?

    _____

    _____

    _____

3   *It is then argued, however, that competitive forces could result in society benefiting from the self-interested behaviour of firms: i. e. that profit maximization will lead to social efficiency under conditions of perfect competition and the absence of externalities.*
    Why is *however* used in this sentence?

    _____

    _____

    _____

4   *But, as we have seen, in the real world, markets are not perfect and there are often considerable externalities.*
    Why does the writer begin the sentence with *But, as we have seen ...?*

    _____

    _____

    _____

5   *In such cases, a lack of social responsibility on the part of firms can have profoundly adverse effects on society.*
    What does *such cases* refer to here?

    _____

    _____

    _____

6   *Indeed, many forms of market failure can be attributed directly to business practices that could not be classified as 'socially responsible': advertising campaigns that seek to misinform or in some way deceive the consumer; monopoly producers exploiting their monopoly position through charging excessively high prices; the conscious decision to ignore water and air pollution limits; knowing that the chances of being caught are slim.*
    Why did the writer use *Indeed* at the beginning of this sentence?

    _____

    _____

    _____

Check your answers with those suggested in the Answer section.

Comment

The argument language, linking words and connectives in this text give the author the means of guiding the reader: it is clear which direction the writer is going in so that the reader can see the step-by-step construction of the argument better. When this is done well, the writer does all the work for the reader, who does not then need to guess what the writer is trying to say. The reader is then in a better position to critically assess the information in the text and form judgements about the information.

4.6 Developing a critical understanding of a reading text

When you 'critically discuss' an essay title, you need to critically read and think about the topic. The best way to do this is to ask yourself questions about the text you are reading. **Asking questions** was one of the active reading skills introduced in Session 2 of this book.

In the next activity you will practise one of the most basic questions you can ask about a reading text to help you critically assess its information or argument. Specifically, you need to decide whether the author presents information in a text as facts that can be checked or opinions that can be argued about. A similar distinction between facts and opinions was introduced in the analysis of essay titles in Session 2.

If you think back to the parts of an argument (see Session 3), very often **data** and **evidence** are **facts** and **claims** and **explanations** are **opinions**. However, as you also saw in Activity 4.8, it is not always that simple to identify parts of arguments. Some explanations or claims are so well accepted that they are almost facts. This is why critical thinking is important. When you think critically, it is useful to remember how much of what people consider is a fact is actually based on opinion.

Activity 4.10 ....

Purpose: to critically assess the claims made by an author.

Task 1: read Text 4.3 in Resource Book 2 again. Then read statements 1 to 5 below. Decide whether the authors of Text 4.3 present the ideas in the statements as **facts** that can be checked or **opinions** that can be argued about.

Task 2: for each statement, identify the particular language (words and expressions) which the authors have used and which helped you make your decision.

1 Firms are only concerned with maximising profits.
   Fact or opinion? Give your reasons:

   _____

   _____

2 Society benefits from competition.
   Fact or opinion? Give your reasons:

   _____

   _____

3 Markets are not perfect in the real world.
   Fact or opinion? Give your reasons:

   _____

   _____

4 A firm with no social responsibility always has a bad effect on society.
   Fact or opinion? Give your reasons:

   _____

   _____

5 There exist marketing campaigns that are dishonest.
   Fact or opinion? Give your reasons:

   _____

   _____

Compare your answers with those suggested in the Answer section.

Comment ....

You can see from these examples how particular words and phrases in texts play an important part in helping you begin to critically analyse the information presented by the author.

In Activity 4.10 you saw the verbs *argued* and *assumed* used to introduce information we should therefore regard as opinion. Other examples of verbs used in source texts in a similar way include:

suggest, claim, maintain, conclude.

You also saw the use of **modal verbs** such as *could* and *can*, which are often associated with opinion. The reason modal verbs are associated with opinion is that they show how strong or how certain the writer is about a statement. If a writer considers their statement to be a fact, and that it is generally accepted as a fact, they are free to make it with a fact verb, such as *is*, for example:

The UK currency is sterling.

However, if a writer knows that a statement is not generally accepted as a fact, either because it is in the future and no one can be sure, or because there are differences of opinion about it, they can show this with a modal verb:

Euro countries may find trading with the UK more difficult than they used to.

The modal verbs that can be used for this purpose are:

may, might, could, should, ought to, can, is able to, would, must.

Modal verbs are like the words *argue* or *claim* because they show that the writer is not presenting the statement as a fact. It is useful to note this when you are reading or writing critically.

For example:

(a)   *Firms are only interested in profits*

is presented as a fact but

(b)   *Firms may only be interested in profits*
(c)   *Firms could only be interested in profits*
(d)   *Firms ought to be interested in profits*

are not presented as facts.

However, if you think about these statements for a moment, you may see that not even (a) is really a fact. It is an opinion. The difference between statement (a) and statements (b)–(d) is that (a) does not seem to recognise that there may be people who have other opinions. On the other hand, statements (b)–(d) are much more open to discussion; they recognise that there are other people who may not agree.

The third way in which a writer can show that a statement is an opinion and not a fact is by using adverbs to modify the statement. In the following example, the adverb *often* makes it clearer that statement (a) is an opinion.

(e)   *Firms are often only interested in profits.*

Critical reading often involves looking out for the ways in which facts are expressed as opinions or opinions are expressed as facts. As a student of business studies, you are expected to be aware that some statements are opinions and others are facts. When you build an argument, you negotiate a way through opinions and facts. Part of the skill of successful argument is to make it clear **how strongly** you are expressing an opinion. The next activity looks at how the writers of Text 4.3 do this.

Activity 4.11   ....

Purpose: to identify examples of language that highlight the **strength** of the writer's claims (making them either stronger or weaker).

Task: identify any language used by the writer of Text 4.3 to strengthen the claims that are made. There are two main types – adverbs and modal verbs. One example of each is identified for you below.

Adverbs used to strengthen or weaken claims	Modal verbs used to strengthen or weaken claims
often	could result

Compare your answers with those suggested in the Answer section.

Comment ....

The most common language used by the writer of this text to strengthen claims is adverbs. They are used to refer to the **extent** of the claim (how much something is **perceived** to be the case). Modal verbs (such as *will, could, could not, can*) also play an important role in making these claims in this text, although you should be careful about how they are interpreted. They appear in sentences that make strong claims, often with the adverbs, for example: ***Indeed**, many forms of market failure **can** be attributed **directly** to business practices that **could not** be classified as 'socially responsible'*. The writer is saying that it is possible to make the connection between business practices and *many forms* of market failure (not all forms), although as you have seen, the language used makes this case quite strongly.

4.7 Critical discussion in writing

So far you have considered how reading texts in certain ways and noticing the language writers use can lead to a deeper understanding of texts. In this section, you will return to the essay title and evaluate some examples of student texts to determine the extent to which the writers use a critical approach. The topic of these texts is another element considered important in the discussion of this title: **public goods**. Text 4.6 in Resource Book 2 is a source text on this topic which the student writers used extensively in their work. However, before you read it, think for a moment about the concept of *public goods*. What does this term mean to you? Can you think of any examples? Why would public goods be relevant to a discussion about market failure and the delivery of socially desirable outcomes? Think about these questions for a minute before reading Text 4.6 in the next activity.

Activity 4.12 ....

Purpose: to evaluate students' summaries of a source text.

Task 1: read Text 4.6 about public goods in Resource Book 2. Then read the three student summaries of this source text, Extracts 4.7 (Mario), 4.8 (Marina) and 4.9 (Peter). Consider how effective the three summaries are. Use the following questions to help you decide.

- Does the summary text include all the important points from the source text?
- Is it accurate?
- Is the text structure effective and the information flow clear?
- Does it create an appropriate relationship with its reader?

Give each text one of the following grades, together with your reasons.

A   A highly effective summary

B   An effective summary overall with some weaknesses

C   An inadequate summary

Mario

Grade (please circle):   A   B   C

Reasons:

_____

_____

_____

_____

Marina

Grade (please circle):   A   B   C

Reasons:

_____

_____

_____

_____

Peter

Grade (please circle):   A   B   C

Reasons:

_____

_____

_____

_____

Task 2: look at the essay-writing checklist in the Appendix at the end of this book. For each comment you have written above, decide which criteria from the essay checklist you are using.

Compare your answers with those suggested in the Answer section.

Comment

Critical discussion in an essay begins with you summarising and paraphrasing the source texts. As you summarise source texts, you are deciding what to select, how you introduce the information you select, how you use the information to build an argument, and how you show your opinion, evaluation and judgement of the information you select and use. As you can see from the suggested answers, success comes from all three sections of the essay-writing checklist. The next activity looks more closely at this.

Activity 4.13

Purpose: to identify features of critical discussion in students' writing.

Task 1: look at the list of features (a)–(g) in the table below. Decide whether each feature is present (✓) or absent (✗) in Marina's text

(Extract 4.8) and Peter's text (Extract 4.9) in Resource Book 2 and note your answers in the table. Use a question mark (?) if you are not sure. **(Note: some features do not appear in either text.)**

Feature	Marina (Extract 4.8)	Peter (Extract 4.9)
(a) Simple summary of sections of the source text		
(b) Support for points being made using direct quotation from the source.		
(c) The student bringing ideas or quotations from other sources to provide additional support or examples of points included in the source text.		
(d) The student expressing an opinion about or giving a personal perspective on ideas in the source text.		
(e) The student providing an explanation of what they understand by a particular key word or phrase from the source text.		
(f) The student providing alternative explanations for a phenomenon or ideas put forward in the source text.		
(g) The student bringing in ideas from other sources that go beyond or call into question the ideas in the source text.		

Task 2: from the list of your responses in the table, which student do you think better fulfils the requirements of the title which asks them to 'critically discuss' the topic?

_____'s text better fulfils the task of critically discussing the topic because …

_____

_____

_____

_____

_____

_____

_____

_____

Compare your answers with those suggested in the Answer section.

Comment

Critical discussion is successful if you can find a basis for questioning what you read. The best way to do this is to read different texts which have different opinions and different arguments. Writers have different opinions because either they have different data and evidence or they have found different explanations. Successful critical discussion essays should do the same. They question claims, point out different evidence and/or present different explanations.

This kind of critical writing relates to three sections of the essay-writing checklist: Section A, which deals with the different source texts you use; Section B, which deals with the way you organise your source materials into a critical discussion text; and Section C, which deals with the language you use in order to succeed in Sections A and B. Next you use these criteria to evaluate some students' critical essays.

4.8 Evaluating students' critical discussion essays

Introductions

The way in which a writer intends to approach a critical discussion of a topic is generally indicated in the introduction to the text. Here you look at some examples of introductions written by students addressing the title you have been considering in this session: 'Critically discuss why markets may fail to deliver socially desirable outcomes.'

As you are aware from Sessions 2 and 3, there are many ways to introduce an academic essay, although most writers seem to include one or more of the following features.

- A link back to the title.
- Give a general background to the topic of the essay; maybe define the topic.
- Identify key concepts that will frame the essay.
- Say what the essay is about by identifying a central claim.
- Give an overview of what the essay contains or how it is structured.

Activity 4.14

Purpose: to evaluate essay introductions.

Task: evaluate the three examples of student introductions in Extracts 4.10, 4.11 and 4.12 of Resource Book 2. Then return to this activity and identify the features of each introduction by putting a tick or a cross in the table below.

Feature	Introduction		
	Alan (Extract 4.10)	Barbara (Extract 4.11)	Marina (Extract 4.12)
A link back to the title			
Give a general background to the topic of the essay			
Define the topic			
Identify key concepts that will frame the essay			
Say what the essay is about by stating a central claim			
Give an overview of what the essay contains or how it is structured			

Compare your answers with those suggested in the Answer section.

Comment ....

Barbara's introduction is the most complex in the sense that it contains more elements than the others. However, it is not necessarily the case that the more elements you include in your introduction, the better it is. The decision about what to include depends very much on what you as the writer think it is necessary or important to include. For example, you may decide that it is necessary to define a term or concept at the beginning of your essay because of its importance in the text as a whole, and because the reader should understand it in a particular way. However, defining terms may not always be necessary, or they may be more appropriate in the body of the text.

Elsewhere, at or near the end of Alan's and Barbara's introduction, they refer to what they will cover in their essays; specifically, the reasons for market failure (Alan's introduction: *There are several reasons why this may fail to happen*; Barbara's introduction: *This paper explores and expands on these causes of market failure.*).

Conclusions

As mentioned in Session 3, the essay-writing checklist refers to the conclusions of essays and so far you have not examined any conclusions. The conclusion is an important part of an essay. It is often the place where a student's critical discussion is most obvious.

The purpose of a conclusion is to ensure that you and your reader are both clear you have answered the question in the essay title.

As Session 3 pointed out, the introduction answers the question: 'What is this essay about?'

The conclusion answers the question: 'What was the point of this essay?'

The conclusion is a good place to reinforce the point of the essay. It can remind the reader what the essay was about – the question in the essay title and the central claim in the introduction; it can summarise the main points in support of the claim; and it can show the added value that the argument in the essay has created (Figure 4.1).

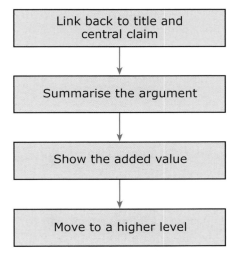

Figure 4.1 Structure of an essay conclusion

Showing added value may mean repeating the claim from the introduction, but now backed up with all the points developed in the essay and summarised in the conclusion, or it may mean moving up to a higher-level viewing platform in the essay. This could mean looking into the future, or taking a more global view, or even pointing out limitations in the research done for the essay and suggesting how it could be done better.

Extract P is an example of this conclusion structure from one of the essays you studied in Session 3 on the impact of Nike in developing countries. The highlighted words are evaluation words.

Extract P

[1] To conclude, **it seems clear that** the introduction of investment by large corporations places them in a position to influence governments, economies and businesses in a developing country that they do not possess in developed countries. [2] This investment **can provide significant benefits** to the state's economic health and wealth which, **albeit often inequitably shared**, can directly improve the lives of its citizens. [3] Where this investment is sustained benefit **is likely to continue**. [4] However, the effect when such large corporations withdraw from a country **can result in** economic decline, unemployment and financial instability.	Link back to title and central claim Summary of argument and added value Higher level

As you can see, the evaluation words show there is judgement and comment in all stages of the conclusion.

Activity 4.15 ....

Purpose: to evaluate essay conclusions.

Task: evaluate the two examples of students' conclusions in Resource Book 2 (Extracts 4.13 and 4.14). Identify any of the features of conclusions discussed above. Then write a brief evaluation.

_____

_____

_____

_____

Compare your answer with that suggested in the Answer section, which also contains the comment.

4.9 Evaluating a full critical discussion essay

The next activity is designed to bring together all you have studied in this session on the failure of markets to deliver socially desirable outcomes and the processes and product of critical essay writing. It is an opportunity to use the essay-writing checklist and become familiar with the criteria it contains. You will use this checklist when writing your assignment over the next two weeks and your tutor will use it to evaluate your writing.

Activity 4.16   ....

Purpose: to critically evaluate a student's assignment.

Task: imagine you have been asked to comment on Text 4.15, a student's assignment, paying particular attention to the extent to which the student has responded critically to the task.

To guide you, use the critical discussion checklist in Activity 4.13 and the essay-writing checklist in the Appendix.

Note the following:

(a) two good points about the student's assignment (be as specific as possible, e.g. give references to the line numbers)

(b) two points about the student's assignment that could be improved (again, be as specific as possible).

4.10 Review

In this session you have critically read several extracts from source texts on the topic of markets and their failure to deliver socially desirable outcomes, and studied the writing of students' critical essays on the subject. In the process you have developed paraphrasing skills, which include selecting appropriate parts of the source text to paraphrase or summarise, and avoiding plagiarism. You examined a number of critical discussion essays, focusing on the structure of the text and the use of the language of argument to manage the information flow in the argument.

One feature of critical discussion that was illustrated is the way it raises questions about claims, explanations or data in arguments. This is often done by using more than one source text, to contrast the opinions of different writers. You saw how argument language is used in critical discussion to negotiate a path through fact and opinion. You also saw how the technical language of business studies and appropriate evaluation language can be used to create your own academic writing style. Finally, you saw how introductions and conclusions frame a successful critical discussion essay.

In Sessions 5 and 6, you will apply what you have studied in other students' essays to your own writing.

4.11 Answer section

Activity 4.1

Component	Notes
Instruction words	First, note that the word 'discuss' appears in this title. This word can be defined as follows: give reasons for and against; investigate and examine by argument. From this definition you can now begin to see how you should think about what is required in constructing your text. In particular, note the expression *examine by argument*. Thus the concept of 'argument' is central to the meaning of the word 'discuss' in this title. Finally, the first word, 'Critically', tells you how to discuss the question.
Key concepts	Clearly, it is important to look at other parts of the title and ask similar questions about what words or expressions mean so that you can 'discuss' the topic directly: for example, the notion of 'why markets may fail'. You could look at this and ask such questions as: • What does 'market failure' mean? • How can markets 'fail to deliver'? The title also includes the expression 'socially desirable outcomes'. Again you may ask such questions as: • What does this expression mean?' • What is the link between socially desirable outcomes and market failure?

Activity 4.2

Task 1

(a) The function of the market in society; (b) a definition; (c) buy a hamburger; (d) prices.

Task 3

(a) A fruit stall; (b) a remote, non-physical one; (c) households, firms and workers; (d) because it is too expensive for the person in the text; (e) market for lunches, labour, wholesale meat and the local market for rented buildings.

Activity 4.3

Externalities

Cause	Effects	Activity	Examples
Market activities	Costs (socially undesirable)	Production	Pollution from firms
		Consumption	Using cars or smoking
	Benefits (socially desirable)	Production	Allowing other firms to access research data
		Consumption	Using public transport

Activity 4.4

Task 1

Problems	Solutions
Paragraphs C, E, F, H	Paragraphs A, B, D, G

Task 2

Heading	Problem	Solution
Protecting people's interests	1 F 2 H	1 B 2 D
Government intervention in the market	E	A
Taxes and subsidies	C	G

Activity 4.5

Extract B

It is often assumed that firms are simply concerned to *maximize profits*: that they are not concerned with *broader issues* of social responsibility. What this assumption means is that firms are only concerned with the interests of shareholders (or managers) and are not concerned for the well-being of the community *at large*. It is then argued, however, that *competitive forces* could result in society benefiting from the self-interested behaviour of firms: i.e. that profit maximization will *lead to* social efficiency under conditions of perfect competition and the absence of externalities. But, as we have seen, in the real world, markets are not perfect and there are often considerable externalities. In such cases, *a lack of* social responsibility on the part of firms can have *profoundly adverse* effects on society. Indeed, many forms of market failure can be *attributed directly* to business practices that could not be classified as 'socially responsible': advertising campaigns that *seek to misinform* or in some way deceive the consumer; monopoly producers *exploiting* their monopoly position through charging excessively high prices; the conscious decision to ignore water and air pollution limits, knowing that the chances of being caught are *slim*.

Activity 4.6

Robin's paragraph	Comments
1 Lack of information and uncertainty can also lead to market failure.	1 This opening sentence clearly identifies the theme of this paragraph.
2 Perfect competition assumes that consumers, firms and factor suppliers have perfect knowledge of costs and benefits – often this is not the case.	2 There is no attempt to paraphrase this sentence from the original text, although 'often this is not the case' are Robin's words and a good point to make here.
3 Consumers may only purchase some products or services once and therefore have no previous experience on which to base their decision, exacerbated by advertising messages and persuasive sales techniques.	3 This is a reasonable attempt to paraphrase the source text, while the link to the role of advertising, although a good point to make, could perhaps have been explained more clearly.
4 Similarly, firms are often ignorant of market opportunities, prices, costs, rival activity, productivity of factors etc.	4 Apart from the connecting word, the rest of the sentence is almost exactly the same as the original.
5 Consumer and organisational decisions made in the absence of sufficient information can often be wrong and result in market failure.	5 This is a good attempt at paraphrasing the final two sentences of the source text. Unfortunately, the reference is made incorrectly (see the reference to the original at the end of Text 4.3).
(Source: Suneja (2000) Understanding Business: Markets)	

Activity 4.7

Extract C	Julie	Tom
may not be aware of	are possibly unaware of	*may not have* the information to be able to equate
Advertising may contribute to people's ignorance by misleading them	information through advertising might be misleading	individuals *could be misled* by peers into thinking

Extract F	Guy
economic	business
expected future conditions	in expectation of future circumstances
many decisions will be taken that in retrospect will be seen to have been wrong.	There is an inevitable element of risk as to the outcome of such decisions.

Activity 4.9

1 *It is often assumed* is argument language which has the effect of presenting the main idea in the paragraph as a general belief held by many people. It is not presented as the author's opinion. *It is often assumed* is different in meaning from the similar expression, *it can be assumed*. This second expression means the writer **does share** the opinion expressed. The difference lies in the use of *often* in the first and the use of *can be* instead of *is* in the second. Usually, when an argument begins with *it is often assumed* the author goes on to question the data or the explanation supporting the assumption.

2 *This assumption* is argument language which refers to the claim in the previous sentence: *firms are simply concerned to maximize profits: that they are not concerned with broader issues of social responsibility. This assumption* is also a linking word group which links the information in the first sentence to this sentence.

3 *However* is a connective word which reinforces the connection between the idea in this sentence of society *benefiting from the self-interested behaviour of firms* and the idea in the previous sentence. The connective word shows that this sentence is **in contrast with** the idea in the first sentence, where firms are said to be *not concerned with broader issues of social responsibility*.

4 In *But, as we have seen* the connecting word is *But* and the argument language is *as we have seen*. The connecting word tells the reader this sentence will be in contrast to the one before. *As we have seen* is argument language which reminds the reader of a previous claim, explanation and/or evidence that the reader would be aware of, and which contradicts the claim outlined in sentence 3. The writer is therefore putting evidence from the real world into place in order to build their argument.

5 *Such cases* are linking words which refer back to the information in the previous sentence: that is, situations in the real world where externalities occur.

6 *Indeed* is a connecting word which prepares the reader for further evidence or explanation of the point made in the previous sentence: that *a lack of social responsibility on the part of firms can have profoundly adverse effects on society. Indeed* tells the reader that the writer has strong grounds for their claim. The evidence is a series of real-world examples.

Activity 4.10

1 **Opinion**: the writer uses the words *often assumed*. Therefore, people do not always think this, according to the writer.

2 **Opinion**: the phrase *It is argued* is used, and people argue about opinions; they try to persuade others to agree with them. Note also the use of *could* – the author is saying that it is possible for society to benefit but not certain.

3   **Fact**: the author presents this as a fact. *Markets are not* perfect: there are no other words or expressions here to suggest that this information should be regarded as an opinion.

4   **Opinion**: the author uses the word *can* to mean this is **possible** but not always true.

5   **Fact**: although there is no evidence to support this statement, this idea is presented as a fact (*seek to misinform or in some way deceive*). Presumably this is based on the idea that it is 'common knowledge' that this is sometimes the case.

Activity 4.11

Adverbs used to strengthen or weaken claims	Modal verbs used to strengthen or weaken claims
often, simply, only, profoundly, excessively, indeed, directly	could result, can have, can be attributed to, could not be classified

Activity 4.12

Mario: grade C or B

Reasons: Mario's text provides only a brief summary of the main points from the source text (checklist A1). It covers the main elements of the topic, explaining how the free market can never provide public goods and includes the features of non-excludability and non-rivalry. However, if the reader is unfamiliar with these terms, this summary could be difficult to understand as these terms are not defined or explained (checklist C2). Furthermore, this summary makes no reference to the role of government in providing these goods (checklist A1). Finally, the evaluation language is conversational and not academic (checklist C6).

Marina: grade A

Reasons: Marina's summary of the source text is much more detailed than Mario's. Several features make it a successful summary of this text.

- Public goods are defined with a well-selected quotation from the source text which is incorporated smoothly into the student's text. (Checklist A1 and A5)

- Examples of these goods are given after the definition. (Checklist C2)

- Important concepts that explain why the market fails to provide public goods are introduced and explained clearly. (Checklist C2)

- A clear link is made to show how the 'socially desirable but privately unprofitable' characteristic of these goods results in market failure to deliver socially desirable outcomes, again using direct quotation effectively within the student text. (Checklist B7)

- The summary is also more comprehensive in that it refers to the role of government in providing public goods. (Checklist A1)

Peter: grade B

Peter's text contains many of the features outlined in Marina's text. Public goods are defined and examples are given (checklist C2). Key terms (*non-excludability* and *non-rivalry*) are explained and the reason why the free market cannot produce these goods is successfully explained (checklist B7). However, it may be argued that this text does not read quite as well as Marina's (checklist B8). The choice of expression is not quite as clear as her text, which makes it more difficult for the reader to understand the text quickly. For example, the meaning of the second sentence may not be immediately apparent without a brief pause for thought (checklist B8).

Activity 4.13

Task 1

Feature	Marina's text	Peter's text
(a) Simple summary of sections of the same text	✓	✓
(b) Support for points being made using direct quotation from the source	✓ (lines 2–3)	✗
(c) The student bringing ideas or quotations from other sources to provide additional support or examples of points included in the source text.	✗	✗
(d) The student gives a personal perspective on or opinion of ideas in the same text.	✗	? (lines 10–17)
(e) The student providing an explanation of what they understand by a particular key word or phrase from the source text.	✗	✗
(f) The student providing alternative explanations for a phenomenon or ideas put forward in the source text.	✗	✗
(g) The student bringing in ideas from other sources that go beyond or call into question the ideas in the source text.	✗	✓

Task 2

Peter's text better fulfils the task of critically discussing the topic because it includes an important feature that is typically associated with critical discussion (g). Although Marina's text is perhaps a better summary of the source text, a key characteristic of Peter's text is how he uses literature from elsewhere to expand on a theme: in this case, the role of government in providing public goods. This literature is used to question the source text's uncritical reference to government providing public goods. This is an important feature of critical discussion. It also highlights the importance of reading several sources on a topic, as they can provide different perspectives or viewpoints which allow you to develop a critical approach to your writing. As a result of reading more widely in this way, and thinking carefully about the claims made in the texts you read, you can include more of the features (a) to (g) in your writing. The text you produce may be considered to be a more effective critical discussion of a topic.

Activity 4.14

Feature	Introduction		
	Alan (Extract 4.10)	Barbara (Extract 4.11)	Marina (Extract 4.12)
A link back to the title	✓	✓	✓
Give a general background to the topic of the essay	✓	✓	✗
Define the topic	✓	✓	✗
Identify key concepts that will frame the essay	✓	✓	✓
Say what the essay is about by stating a central claim	✓	✓	✗
Give an overview of what the essay will contain or how it will be structured.	✗	✓	✓

Activity 4.15

Both conclusions can be seen to contain typical elements of conclusions, namely:

- a brief summary or restatement of the main points, demonstrating the added value
- a final comment and/or judgement.

Clearly, Peter's conclusion is a much more detailed summary of the issues that were discussed in the body of the essay, although this is not necessarily a better option. Ideally, the conclusion should have only a summary element and not repeat the content in the body in the same level of detail. At the same time, it is a good idea to have enough detail in the summary to leave the reader with a clear reminder of the issues that were discussed. The final sentences of both conclusions work well in terms of bringing together the various issues into a final comment or judgement.

SESSION 5 Writing a 'costs and benefits' essay

5.1 Introduction

The purpose of the final two sessions of this book is to put into practice the communication skills that you have studied in the first four sessions. By the end of Session 6, you will have made preparations to produce a successful essay. This essay will be similar to the one you produce as an assignment for this course.

As with all the student essays you have studied in this course, your essay will be the output of a production process. To some extent, you will be guided through that process in these two sessions. During the process you will revise skills and knowledge that you have already developed in the course, practise new communication skills and develop new business studies knowledge.

The essay focuses on a multinational company takeover. In order to complete this essay, you will read several texts dealing with this area of business studies and apply the concepts learned to case study material describing the takeover. In the essay you will examine the costs and benefits of the takeover. To do this, you will use the essay-writing skills of describing, explaining and critically discussing the impact of the takeover. These are the communication skills that you have practised throughout this book.

Your assignment will be assessed for the business studies knowledge you develop in the process of writing it and for the professional communication skills you use in this process. To assess your assignment, your tutor will use the essay-writing checklist that you have referred to throughout Sessions 2 to 4.

However, the main purpose of the essay-writing checklist is for you to evaluate your own writing as you produce your work. Like any assignment, producing it is a learning process as well. Throughout this session and the next, there are activities designed to reinforce the skills and knowledge that you have already developed, together with activities introducing new ones. All of these activities will support you in producing a successful essay at the end of the process and, equally importantly, in becoming a successful *essay writer*.

A successful essay writer has the skills to interpret the context they are communicating in, adapt their communication to the context, and successfully engage with their audience. These are similar to the professional communication skills needed to succeed in workplace writing.

Learning outcomes

In this session, you will:

- apply the skills practised in previous sessions
- read source texts in preparation for an assessed essay on the costs and benefits of a multinational takeover
- develop business studies knowledge and language relating to multinational corporations and their takeover of other companies
- produce outlines and mind maps for the essay
- produce a first draft of the essay
- develop your understanding of the essay-writing checklist, particularly Section C, 'Control of academic writing style'.

The essay will draw on the business studies knowledge that you have already worked with in this course, including multinational corporations in general and their investment in other countries in particular (Sessions 2 and 3), as well as markets (Session 4). In preparation for the essay, you will extend your knowledge of these areas and work with new knowledge relevant to multinational corporations, including, for example, growth strategy.

5.2 The sample assignment

This sample assignment is based on the case study of the takeover of Asda, a UK-based superstore, by Wal-Mart, a US-based multinational.

Below is a sample title of the assignment, together with some guidance notes. These two short texts are the first inputs to the essay-writing process in this session and the next.

Assignment title

Wal-Mart is a US-based multinational corporation. Critically discuss the likely costs and benefits of its takeover of Asda, a UK-based company.

Notes

This title raises a broad set of issues about markets. These issues are discussed in various texts that you have already read or will read in this session and Session 6. The text, 'Multinational corporations', which is concerned with why businesses go multinational, is particularly relevant. However, the essay title enables you to draw on other texts and make connections between them as you think appropriate.

As you work through the following activities, you may find that there is less feedback in the Answer section than usual. There are three reasons for this.

1   At this point you are expected to have a more developed understanding of the processes involved in essay writing, so you should need less feedback to guide you.

2   The activities in this session will guide you in writing the type of essay that you will submit for assessment at the end of Session 6.

3   By now, you might have decided that you want to adapt the processes introduced in this course to suit your own writing processes. You should feel free to do this and not be constrained by the procedures suggested in the feedback.

Sessions 5 and 6, therefore, will give you enough guidance to be supportive but not so much that your final essay has been written more by the authors of this book than by you.

In the first activity you will think about your preferred way to produce the assignment.

Activity 5.1 ....

Purpose: to think about your preferred procedure for producing a successful essay.

Task: write a brief action plan of the procedure you would follow to produce this essay. This is only an introductory activity and you should not spend very long on it.

Compare your answer with that suggested in the Answer section.

Comment ....

The purpose of this activity was to give you a starting point for reflecting on the essay-writing process as you work through the following activities. As you do them, compare the process you are asked to carry out with the procedure you outlined here. There may be differences between the way you would like to produce this assignment and the activities you are asked to do. It is important to recognise that there are different ways to produce a final essay and that these can be equally successful.

Processing the assignment title and the guidance notes

In Activity 5.1 you outlined your preferred procedure for producing this assignment. The activities in this session will follow the procedure introduced in earlier sessions – particularly in Session 2. As you work through these activities, you should consider how effective you find them, and noting any times when you would prefer to use a different approach. To begin the process, you will focus closely on the assignment title in the way introduced in Session 2.

Activity 5.2 ....

Purpose: to identify the tasks and the knowledge indicated by the assignment title.

Task 1: use the skills introduced in previous sessions to analyse the assignment title given at the beginning of this section.

Write your analysis of the assignment title in your Learning Journal using two columns with the following headings.
- What does the title expect me to **do**?
- What **key concepts** does the title expect me to deal with?

Task 2: complete the mind map in Figure 5.1 with the key concepts referred to in the title. (This is not a brainstorming activity so you should only include the key concepts from the title.) If this mind map is not drawn in the way you would draw one, draw another one that suits you better.

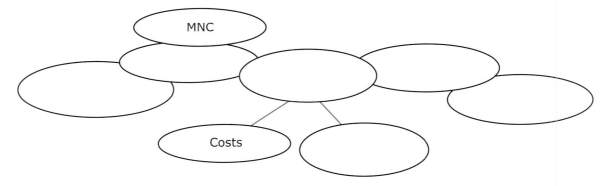

Figure 5.1   For use with Activity 5.2

Task 3: read the guidance notes below the assignment title at the beginning of this section. Then add any new concepts or additional tasks to the two lists in your Learning Journal and to the mind map.

Compare your answers with those suggested in the Answer section.

Comment ....

Tasks 1 and 2 apply the skills that you practised in Sessions 2 to 4. However, processing this title highlights a pair of concepts which have not been examined before but are important for the design of this essay – *costs* and *benefits*. These are considered more fully next.

The assignment title and the design of an essay

Session 3 introduced the idea of designing an essay. The design depends on the purpose of the essay. This is indicated in the assignment title. In the previous activity, you identified what this assignment title asks you to do. In the next activity, you will think about how you should design the essay to achieve this. That activity addresses the first criterion in Section B of the essay-writing checklist: 'Text structure is appropriate to the task'.

Like the assignment title in Session 4, this one asks you to *critically discuss* a situation. Session 4 introduced the design of a critical discussion. However, the way you design a critical discussion depends on what you are discussing. Critically discussing the failure of markets to produce socially desirable outcomes – as you did in Session 4 – will be organised in a different way from the critical discussion of the costs and benefits of a *takeover*.

As preparation for your reading in this session, the next activity focuses on the design of the essay that you will produce. The concepts of *costs* and *benefits* are introduced in two paragraphs. These discuss each concept in relation to a multinational company's investment in a developing country (called the *host nation* or *host economy* in this extract). You are already familiar with this topic through your reading on the influence of Nike on a developing economy in Sessions 2 and 3.

Activity 5.3   ....

Purpose: to think about the design of a 'costs and benefits' discussion essay.

Task 1: the verbs and nouns below come from the text you will read about the *costs* and *benefits* when a multinational company invests in a developing country. Before you read the text, guess which words come from the costs paragraph and 'which ones' are from the benefits paragraph. One example is given for each paragraph to get you started.

raise	destroy	bring in	pose problems	stimulate induce
increase uncertainty	promote	insecurity		repatriate profits

Costs	Benefits
Destroy	Stimulate

Task 2: now read Extract A below to check whether your guesses were correct. It is not necessary to understand every word in the extract to do this. You may find that some of your guesses were wrong. If so, explain why.

Extract A

[Paragraph 1]

MNCs may potentially bring a lot of benefits to the host nation. They may raise the growth rate of the host nation by bringing in new investment, new technologies or managerial competencies. They may stimulate inter-firm competition and thereby induce their domestic rivals to become more innovative and competitive. MNCs may also promote the development of various supporting industries or complementary industries.

[Paragraph 2]

MNCs may, however, also bring in several costs for the host economy. Sometimes MNCs may enjoy such a huge competitive advantage over local firms that they can destroy local competition rather than promoting it. At other times, they may not promote the development of any local economic activity but simply source their components from abroad. They may repatriate most of their profits rather than reinvesting them in the domestic economy. MNCs may also pose serious regulatory problems for host governments because of their 'footloose' nature. Their ability to relocate their activities internationally may also increase uncertainty and insecurity for a nation's workforce. Multinationals may also be able to avoid paying their due share of taxes to national governments by practising transfer pricing.

Task 3: now answer the following comprehension questions. Note that (a)–(e) are on paragraph 1 and (f)–(k) are on paragraph 2.

(a) Paragraph 1 is about several organisations. Sentence 1 names two: *MNCs* and *the host nation*. Which other organisations are named in the paragraph?

(b) Paragraph 1 deals with several cause–effect relationships. One effect mentioned is a rise in the growth rate of the host nation. Which of the following factors may cause such a rise: *complementary industries*, *MNC investment*, *domestic rivals*, *new technologies*, *managerial competencies*?

(c) Another cause–effect relationship in paragraph 1 involves three factors in a cause–effect relationship. Two of them are *MNC investment* and *more innovative and competitive domestic companies*. What is the third factor in the relationship?

(d) Think about Nike and give an example of a *supporting industry* and a *complementary industry*. Use a dictionary, if necessary, to decide on the meanings of these two noun groups.

(e) Draw a cause–effect diagram for all the cause–effects in paragraph 1, using boxes to show the causes and effects. You may need to make noun groups for each box by combining words from the paragraph. Join the boxes with arrows to show what the cause is and what the effect is. Remember, some effects may have more than one cause. The first sentence is done in Figure 5.2 as an example.

Figure 5.2 For use with Activity 5.3, Task 3

(f) Paragraph 2 begins with a claim. What is it in your own words?

(g) The cause–effect diagram in Figure 5.3 provides data that supports the claim in the first sentence of the paragraph. Referring to paragraph 2, explain why this cause–effect happens.

Figure 5.3 For use with Activity 5.3, Task 3

(h) Referring to paragraph 2, write an explanation of the cause–effect in Figure 5.4.

Figure 5.4 For use with Activity 5.3, Task 3

(i) Referring to paragraph 2, write an explanation of the cause–effect in Figure 5.5.

Figure 5.5 For use with Activity 5.3, Task 3

(j) Referring to paragraph 2, write an explanation of the cause–effect in Figure 5.6.

Figure 5.6 For use with Activity 5.3, Task 3

(k) Each explanation you have given in questions (h)–(j) can be expressed as a noun group. For example, the explanation for (g) is *the huge competitive advantage of MNCs over local firms*. Do the same for the remaining explanations.

Now look at the answers for Tasks 1–3 in the Answer section.

Task 4: the mini essay outlines below will help you think about the design of the essay you are going to write. None of these designs is exactly right for the assignment as it is, but together they give some ideas which may help you develop your own design.

Look through the four designs. Identify **any part** of any design that you think will be appropriate for this assignment and make a note of it. When you have selected these parts, try to combine all the ones you think are suitable into an outline for your essay. The purpose of the activity is to **start thinking** about design and how you will organise your essay.

Introduction
Wal-Mart and Asda
Main body
Definition of *MNC* and *takeover* History of events leading up to takeover
Conclusion

Introduction
Takeovers Central claim about costs and benefits
Main body
Costs 1 Claim–Explanation–Data **Costs 2, etc.** **Benefits 1** Claim–Explanation–Data **Benefits 2, etc.**
Conclusion

Introduction
Types of costs and benefits
Main body
Cost 1 Generalisation Examples and details from case study **Cost 2 Generalisation** Examples and details from case study **Benefit 1 Generalisation** Examples and details from case study **Benefit 2 Generalisation** Examples and details from case study
Conclusion

Introduction
Wall-Mart and Asda
Main body
Descriptions of the two companies History of events since takeover
Conclusion

There is no answer suggested for this task because it is part of your preparation for the essay.

Comment

One purpose of this activity was to encourage you to think about the elements that will go into the design of the essay that you will produce. Perhaps the most important aspect of the design of a costs and benefits essay is that it looks at the **positive** and the **negative** effects of an event.

When you think about essay design, you consider the structure and development of the text (Section B of the essay-writing checklist). As the last task in this activity showed, this may involve bringing together parts from several essay designs at the same time. You should decide this for yourself during the essay-writing process.

5.3 Preparing to read

In this section, the main focus is on reading source material for this essay. Activities 5.1, 5.2 and 5.3 have already raised questions about the essay. However, as Session 2 suggests, to read effectively, it is important to have clear questions you are trying to answer, which are directly related to the essay title.

Activity 5.4

Purpose: to develop questions before reading.

Task: look back at the essay title and the mind map in Activity 5.1 and think about the ideas you had in Activities 5.2 and 5.3. Make a list of questions that might help you read the source material most effectively.

There is no suggested answer for you to compare with yours. The purpose of this activity is for you to decide which questions are important for you.

The guidance notes for the assignment suggest that a range of source texts are relevant to this title. The next activity asks you to think about some of the source texts that might be useful.

Activity 5.5

Purpose: to make some decisions about the kind of texts to read for this sample assignment.

Task: keeping the assignment title, the guidance notes and your questions in mind, read the list of source materials below. Which do you think will be most useful or relevant? Write 1 against the most relevant text, 2 against the next most important text, and so on. As you do not have the actual texts to look at, and you have not yet read very much on this subject, don't spend long on this activity. Make your judgements on the basis of your first impressions.

(a) Sloman, J. and Sutcliffe, M. (2000) 'Multinational corporations', in Suneja, V. (ed.) *Understanding Business: Markets*, London, Routledge, pp. 196–212.

(b) Costello, N. (2000) 'Organisations', in Suneja, V. (ed.) *Understanding Business: Markets*, London, Routledge, pp. 83–114.

(c) Hobsbawm, E (2000) 'The British industrial revolution', in Suneja, V. (ed.) *Understanding Business: Markets*, London, Routledge, pp. 37–55.

(d) Brown, V. (1991) 'Competition and power in markets', in Suneja, V. (ed.) *Understanding Business: Markets*, London, Routledge, pp. 117–44.

(e) Wal-Mart's annual report

(f) Whysall, P. (2001) 'Wal-Mart's takeover of Asda: what the papers said', *British Food Journal*, vol. 103, no. 10, pp. 729–43.

(g) Suneja, V. (2000). *Study Guide for the Course: Understanding Business Behaviour: Markets*, Milton Keynes, The Open University Business School.

(h) Open University Business School (2006) *Asda Wal-Mart Case Study*, Milton Keynes, The Open University.

Compare your answers with those suggested in the Answer section.

Comment ....

As the answer suggests, your decision about the usefulness and order in which you read these texts depends partly on your own preference and partly on what the texts actually contain. The main point of this activity is to highlight that an essay-writing assignment may involve reading several texts rather than just one.

Before reading some of the business studies texts suggested, the next two activities ask you to consider some of the less academic knowledge that you already have, or could easily find about the topic of this sample assignment. The first one looks at the evidence for MNC activity in your own everyday life.

Activity 5.6 ....

Purpose: to recognise some of the evidence for multinational company (MNC) activity in your everyday life and to relate it to the assignment title.

Task: consider some of the manufactured products in your house (for example, the toothpaste and shampoo in your bathroom and the television in your living room). Think about the following questions and consider whether there is any link between these products and the assignment title.

1   Which company produced them?

2   Where were they produced? If they were not produced in your country, why do you think this is?

3   Were they cheaper than other brands? Was this a factor in your decision to buy them? What other factors influenced your choice?

There are no suggested answers for these questions but they are discussed in the comment below.

Comment ....

This is a thinking activity which focuses on the products of MNCs. Your T-shirt may have been bought in a UK store but its label says 'made in the Philippines'. Your television may bear the logo of a Japanese company but it was manufactured in Taiwan. Think back to the assignment title. Why do companies prefer to produce their goods outside their home country? Various factors, such as the cost of production, the nature of the workforce, market demands, government regulations and technology affect how MNCs operate in today's world. The expansion of MNCs may have both benefits and costs – for the companies, for their customers, employees and suppliers, and for the countries in which they operate.

Although a discussion of the products in your home is not appropriate in a business studies essay, making connections with your own experience can contribute to a better understanding of the academic texts you will read.

5.4 Reading about multinational companies

For most of the rest of this session you will read about multinational companies. The readings are relevant to the essay you will write. However, unlike the activities in previous sessions, most of the activities in this section do not focus specifically on that sample assignment.

The following activities have two purposes:

1   to introduce business studies **knowledge** that you can use for writing the assignment

2   to develop business studies **language** for writing the assignment.

Business studies language is dealt with in Section C of the essay-writing checklist, 'Control of academic writing style'. The following activities are designed to develop your understanding and control of the business studies language in two texts. This requires you to read the texts more closely than you might normally do. You may sometimes find this close reading unusual, so it is important to remember the two purposes mentioned above. You may also find some answers seem rather obvious. Again this is because the purpose of the question is to focus your attention as much on the **words** that are used to communicate the ideas as on the ideas themselves.

Good readers do not stop to pay attention to the words in this way. If there is a word they do not understand fully, they often carry on reading without stopping. These activities ask you to note the use of words rather than simply understand the ideas. This is also why you are asked to write out the answers to these tasks. Writing is more active than silent reading and is another way of reinforcing your awareness of how words are used.

Activity 5.7   ....

Purpose: to develop some general concepts and vocabulary for discussing multinational corporations.

Task 1: Reading

Text 5.1 in Resource Book 2 is a four-paragraph text called 'Multinational corporations – an introduction'. This activity will raise some questions about this introductory text, in preparation for reading a more detailed text on the same subject of multinational corporations. For some of the tasks in this activity, you are asked to think about some details that are **not** in this introductory text. Here, you should use your existing knowledge, or look in an online or a printed business dictionary or other reference text, if required. For some tasks, you may feel you can't provide the details you are asked for. It is acceptable to write that in your answer.

Write down your responses to the following.

1   Before you look at Text 5.1, based on its title and length, what aspects of multinational corporations do you expect it to cover? Write down some key concepts.

2   Turn to Text 5.1 and read quickly **the beginning sentences of each paragraph only**. Write a one-word summary for each paragraph.

3   Read the whole text more closely to see whether the key concepts you predicted in question 1 are in the text.

4   Why do some companies do business overseas by simply exporting goods and services?

5   Choose one of the four features that make multinational companies so diverse. Write an explanation of this feature for someone who may not understand it.

6   Write a **definition** of *turnover* and *GDP* which **compares multinational companies** and **countries**.

7   Explain how going multinational could lead to a reduction in costs for a firm.

8   Do you think exploiting an advantage over a rival is a *cause* or an *effect* of growth?

9   Give an example of a fixed cost that would illustrate *economies of scale*.

10 Give an example of an *import restriction* which might motivate a firm to go multinational.

11 Four problems of going multinational are mentioned. It is possible to group the four problems into two pairs of similar problems. How would you divide up the problems to make two similar pairs?

Compare your answers with those suggested in the Answer section.

Comment ....

Most of these questions ask you to focus on the specialised business words that are used in Text 5.1. It is usually easier to read a text if you don't stop to explain all the terms in it; but explaining the terms that you use is an important aspect of essay writing. This task provides practice in doing this for the business studies words that might be useful in the essay you will write on Wal-Mart's takeover of Asda.

The next task concentrates on how business studies words are often used in fixed combinations in business studies texts. These fixed combinations are not the same as the word groups you studied in earlier activities. Often they combine words from different word groups. For example, they may combine verbs with noun groups. Developing control of common business studies word combinations is part of developing successful professional communication skills.

Task 2: Language focus – word combinations

The words in the table below are from Text 5.1. They are mixed up but they normally occur together in word combinations that are common in business studies.

Without looking back at Text 5.1, match one word or word group from the left-hand column with one word or word group in the right-hand column. Some of the words in the left-hand column may be used more than once. Check your answers by finding the original combinations in Text 5.1.

to export	productive assets
to jump	superior technology
labour	managerial expertise
foreign	foreign assets
ownership of	assets
costs	assets
transport	goods or services
to spread	a turnover that exceeds £100 billion
to circumvent	in costs
fixed	costs
reduction	costs
to have	costs
productive	costs
to exploit	of raw materials
to suffer	a competitive advantage
to locate	economies of scale
	diseconomies of scale
	operations
	tariff barriers
	import restrictions

Compare your answers with those suggested in the Answer section.

Comment ....

To some extent, when you study business you are learning how words go together. For example, *economies of scale* is a specialised business studies noun group. If you know how to use it, it will help you to explain why companies go multinational. But it will not be enough on its own. You may also need to know that it combines with the verb *exploit* and that it does not combine with other verbs like *use* or *have*. You may also need to know that *exploit* has a positive meaning when used with *economies of scale* but a negative meaning when used with cheap labour, for example. It may also be useful to know that there is an opposite word group – *diseconomies of scale*. Finally, it may be useful to know that a company does not *exploit diseconomies of scale* but it *suffers* them. These are all examples of how word combinations are part of learning about business.

In the next activity you will work with a more detailed text on the subject of multinational corporations. As you work with this text, links will be made to the work you did on the introductory text in Activity 5.7. Again, the focus is on the language used, as well as the meaning of the text.

Activity 5.8

Purpose: to extend the concepts and vocabulary that were introduced in Activity 5.7.

Task 1:

1   In Activity 5.7, you wrote a summary word for each of the four paragraphs in Text 5.1. Look at the section headings and subheadings in Text 5.2 and match each summary word from Text 5.1 to a section or subsection of Text 5.2. From the section headings of Text 5.2, does it seem to include any aspects of multinational companies that are not covered by Text 5.1?

2   Read through the section 'What is a multinational corporation?', to get a general impression of what it is about. Is the information in this section organised in the same order as the information in paragraph 1 of Text 5.1?

What is a multinational corporation?

3   Which two features of *diversity* in Text 5.2 are not covered in Text 5.1?

4   According to Text 5.2, what is wrong with the definition of an MNC given in Text 5.1? **Paraphrase the words used in the text.**

5   What other word group does Text 5.2 use to mean *productive asset in a foreign country*?

6   Text 5.1 refers to the *nature of an MNC's business*. In Text 5.2 there is also another word group for this concept. What is it?

7   What other word groups does Text 5.2 use for GDP?

8   What kind of business is a **typical** MNC business?

9   In one sentence, explain the factors that influence how MNCs decide on their *production location*. Don't give an example, just make a generalisation.

10 There are two main kinds of ownership patterns. Why might a company choose a particular pattern?

11 One kind of organisation structure is where subsidiaries are *self-standing*. What is the other?

12 Write a paraphrase of the two types of organisation structure in question 11 without using any of the words from the text except *MNC*. Is your paraphrase written in an academic style? Are there any words from the text which you think are absolutely necessary for writing about organisation structure because they are specialised business studies vocabulary?

Compare your answers with those suggested in the Answer section.

Comment ....

Once again, the questions in this task have focused on the business studies words for discussing MNCs. The paraphrasing questions show how paraphrasing involves a careful selection between specialised words which are useful because they communicate effectively and other words which are necessary to avoid copying the source text.

Task 2:

Multinational corporations and the UK economy

1   What is the point of the information in the section 'Multinational corporations and the UK economy'? Write one sentence to answer this question.

Categories of multinational

2   Write a two or three-sentence description of each type of MNC in your own words. The sentences should define each type, explain why each one is created and, in two cases, give an example. You should use specialised words or word combinations from the source text that you think are necessary to communicate effectively and other words that you think are necessary to avoid plagiarism.

3   In the following summarising sentence, fill in the gaps in brackets with the names of the different types of MNC.

MNCs can be divided into those that are using their multinational base primarily as a means of achieving growth [_____ _____] and those that are using it to reduce costs [_____ _____].

Why do businesses go multinational?

4   Why does a section called 'Why do businesses go multi-national?' begin with a half-page discussion about different types of MNC?

Compare your answers with those suggested in the Answer section.

Comment ....

These questions continue the practice of paraphrasing and using specialised language. Once again this raises questions about which words and word combinations are necessary in order to communicate effectively and which ones you should consider changing. When paraphrasing the information on the three types of MNC, it is not useful to change their names because they are generally recognised key concepts from business studies.

Some ideas can be expressed in different words which have more or less the same meaning. In the suggested answer to (2), *manage risk* is used instead of *spread risk*. *Risk* is a specialised word – a key concept – which is necessary for this paraphrase. The most precise combination is the original one – *spread risk*. *Manage risk* is used in the paraphrase in order to avoid using the original words. It does not have exactly the same meaning but is close enough for this context. The point is that paraphrasing is a process of using words and word combinations from the source text when they are particularly effective and using other words and word combinations if possible.

In some cases a particular word combination is especially suited to expressing an idea and it is difficult to find another that would express it as effectively. An example is the word combination *achieve growth by expanding into new markets*. The paraphrase that is suggested – to *grow through expansion into different markets* – uses a similar combination but the word forms have been changed. The noun *growth* has become the verb *grow* and the verb *expanding* has become the noun *expansion*. Changing nouns into verbs or vice versa is a common way of paraphrasing. It shows that sometimes the original word combination is so effective that it is almost impossible to find better words.

If you try to think of other words that might replace the verb *expanding* in the word combination above, it is difficult to think of a better one:

*achieve growth by **growing** into new markets*

*achieve growth by **moving** into new markets*

*achieve growth by **entering** into new markets*

are possibilities, but they are not better. The first one is repetitive and the other two do not really have the same meaning. There are other words with the same meaning as *expanding*, such as *increasing*, *enlarging* and *extending*, but they do not make sense in this combination.

This does not mean that you should not attempt to paraphrase; but it does show that paraphrasing requires particular skill.

Task 3:

Reductions in costs

1   With reference to this section, name three factors of production.

2   Write an explanation of how factors of production lead to the establishment of multinationals. Write this by moving from a high-level generalisation down to lower-level details. Start with a generalisation about factors of production, then write a lower-level generalisation about labour, followed by an example.

3   Using the concept of *cost conditions*, explain how Nike organises its production globally.

4   The UK is 'the largest recipient of inward direct investment after Canada' (Sloman and Sutcliffe, 2000, p. 200). Use the concepts of *factor quality* and *cost per unit of output* to write an explanation of this. How sure are you about this explanation? Write a claim that shows how sure you are. Use a reference to support your claim.

5   Explain in your own words how going multinational would reduce transport costs. Apart from the concept of *transport costs*, which key business concepts have you used in your explanation? Which words from the text have you paraphrased by putting them into your own words?

6   Text 5.1 uses the expression *circumvention of import restrictions*. What equivalent expression does Text 5.2 use?

7   What do government incentives do?

8   Describe how one of the three government incentives mentioned works.

Compare your answers with those suggested in the Answer section.

Comment ....

The questions in Task 3 ask you to produce some slightly longer output texts. These show how key concepts and word combinations (which are both criteria in Section C of the essay-writing checklist) interact with paragraph organisation (which is covered in Section B of the checklist).

In question 2, it is probably better to call the text you produce a **summary** rather than a **paraphrase** as it has used far fewer words than the source text – particularly in the Nike example which is a whole paragraph in the original. There are many different ways of expressing the ideas in this. However, the paragraph organisation is fairly typical, moving from a high-level generalisation to lower-level details. It is possible to give more details but this is not necessary for this particular paragraph. Once again, the output text is a mix of specialised business language from the original text and paraphrase using other specialised business language, word combinations from other business studies texts, and other words from the writer's mind.

Another output paragraph is produced in question 3. Costs and cost conditions are key concepts that link the information in this paragraph. The opening sentence makes *Nike*, *production* and *cost conditions* the themes of the paragraph. They are what the paragraph is about. The following sentences explain the generalisation in the theme sentence. This is the point of the paragraph.

The paragraph for question 4 uses several business studies concepts to make a convincing claim. The claim is introduced in the first sentence, explained in the second sentence, and then made again in the final sentence. The explanation makes the claim convincing. The claim is also supported by the reference to Sloman and Sutcliffe, who are two recognised business studies writers. Section A of the essay-writing checklist covers how skilfully you use the source material and how you reference it to support claims like this effectively.

Task 4:

Growth strategy

1 *Growth strategy* is the concept which frames this section of the discussion of MNCs. What are the two general effects of becoming multinational? Would you try to paraphrase these two effects if you were including them in an assignment? Or would you use the word combinations from the source text?

2 The second effect is subdivided into three subcategories. What are they?

3 Each of the three subcategories you have just listed is also a cause. Write each subcategory as a cause–effect sentence.

Compare your answers with those suggested in the Answer section.

Comment ....

The purpose of a company strategy is to have effects in the real world. For this reason, cause-effect analysis is an important part of the explanation of why a company adopts a strategy.

Task 5:

The product life cycle and the multinational company

1 For each phase in the product life cycle, write a single cause–effect sentence to explain what happens in that phase.

2 Paraphrase the sentence in this section which makes **the main generalisation** about product life cycle and the MNC. Remember that main generalisations can come at the beginning of a text when they say what the text is about, or at the end when they say what point the text was making. You can

paraphrase only a single sentence in this section. Which one will you choose? Try not to use any words from the original source text when you paraphrase it. Note, however, when you **have to use** one of the words from the source text because there is no other way of expressing the same idea.

Compare your answers with those suggested in the Answer section.

Comment

As with many business studies texts, the main purpose of this text is to explain what happens by describing causes and effects. Key concepts such as the *phases in the life cycle of a product* are explained in this way. As you may have noticed, this explanation is described as a *hypothesis*. The generalisation which you paraphrased in question 2 is a claim made by business studies writers. It is an opinion and the four phases described are the explanation of the hypothesis. What is needed to complete this argument is some real-world data that could support the claim and the explanation but that is not given in this text.

Most of the claim can be paraphrased except for some key words, such as *production*, *location*, *profits* and *product*. As with all paraphrasing, you need to use a mix of the specialist terminology and other words to produce an academic style that can be called 'your own words'.

Task 6:

Problems facing multinationals

1   Explain why the problem of language is greater in developing countries.

2   Create a key concept that summarises the problem of selling and marketing in foreign markets.

3   Create a key concept that summarises the behaviour of some host governments.

4   Explain *diseconomies of scale* by reference to *communication* and *control*.

Compare your answers with those suggested in the Answer section.

Comment

The source text does not give a clear explanation for question 1, so the suggested answer is not presented as a fact but as a claim. This is shown by the use of *perhaps* in the explanation. When using source texts as the basis of arguments, it is important to reference them correctly. This is covered in Section A of the essay-writing checklist.

Neither of the two suggested answers for questions 2 and 3 is in the source text. These are examples of key concepts from other texts or from the writer's own mind. They are the writer's 'own words' because they are not copied from the source text; but, of course, they are not words that the writer has invented. They are still examples of the academic writing style which is evaluated in Section C of the essay-writing checklist.

The suggested answer to question 4 is an example of how business studies texts use key concepts and arrange them into particular relationships – often of cause and effect – to explain what happens in business. When summarised explanations such as these are used in essays, they satisfy many of the criteria in Sections A, B and C of the essay-writing checklist.

Conclusion

Texts 5.1 and 5.2 are two of the recommended texts for this sample assignment. In the activities in this section, you focused closely on ideas about multinational corporations and the language used to communicate those ideas. You also wrote small texts, some of which may prove useful for this assignment. However, throughout these activities you have not been asked to make connections between the reading you have done and the essay you will write. You will do this in the next activity. In the following section you will read a case study of Wal-Mart's takeover of Asda.

5.5 Reading the Asda Wal-Mart case study

The assignment task you are working with expects students to read the kind of business studies texts you explored in Section 5.4. It also expects them to read a case study. You will read that case study in this section.

The assignment production process

As the success of an essay depends very much on what you read and how you read it, it is important that you are clear about what you are being asked to do. So far in this session you have read two input texts which contain concepts relevant to the assignment title. At this point you have two choices.

1   You may choose to re-read Texts 5.1 and 5.2, looking particularly for ideas that are relevant to the essay you will write. Then you need to read the case study text to focus on what happened in the Wal-Mart Asda takeover. You may then want to re-read all the texts again.

2   You may choose to read the case study text first. Then you need to re-read Texts 5.1 and 5.2. You will probably then need to re-read all three texts again.

The texts are presented in a particular sequence below but it is up to you which sequence you follow. The important point is that you will probably need to read all the texts several times to develop **a framework for analysing the case study** and **an outline for writing the essay**. In this section, you will concentrate on framing the case study. In the next section, you will concentrate on outlining the essay.

Before you look at the case study, here are the six case-study analysis skills introduced in Book 1:

1   Mapping the case
2   Framing the case
3   Recognising influences and impacts (or cause–effects)
4   Identifying problems
5   Proposing solutions
6   Evaluating the analysis.

You must decide which of these skills are important for the essay. For this section, you should pay particular attention to the first two.

In the next activity you will **map the case**. After you have done this, you will read the case again in order to **frame it**.

Activity 5.9

Purpose: to map the case study.

Task: using the active reading skills, which were reintroduced in Session 2 of this book, read the Asda Wal-Mart case study (Text 5.3 of Resource Book 2) and produce a map or an overview of it.

There are no suggested answers for this activity because it is part of the preparation for your essay.

Comment

In essay writing, a case study like this provides data, evidence and examples from the business world. The academic texts you read earlier (Texts 5.1 and 5.2) provide the business studies concepts, models and theories for framing this data.

In the next activity you will spend some time organising the framework you will need to frame the case study. Activity 5.3 highlighted the fact that this essay is a costs and benefits essay and that costs are negative effects and benefits are positive effects. Costs and benefits are the basis of the framework you develop next.

Activity 5.10

Purpose: to decide the framework you will use to frame the case study.

Task: look back at the mind map, the essay design plans and the questions you produced in Activities 5.2 to 5.4 to remind yourself of the sample assignment title and your first thoughts about the title.

Now create a table on your computer (using the 'landscape' setting for the paper rather than the 'portrait' or lengthwise setting). Write the title of the assignment at the top of the page. Then insert a table with two columns and up to 10 rows. For one column heading write 'Benefits (positive effects)' and for the other column write 'Costs (negative effects)', so that your table looks like this.

Wal-Mart is a US-based multinational corporation. Critically discuss the likely costs and benefits of its takeover of Asda, a UK-based company.

Benefits (positive effects)	Costs (negative effects)

Then read Texts 5.1 and 5.2 again. Your purpose is to build a framework to use when you read the case study. You will have to read the texts critically as they do not generally refer to the concept 'takeover', which is a key concept in the case study. You will have to make links between the texts and the assignment title.

This is a note-making activity. You should make notes in the following three ways.

1   Using the active reading methods described in Session 2, highlight anything that is important in the texts.

2   On a separate sheet of paper, make notes using the note-making methods introduced in Session 2.

3   Either afterwards or at the same time, write key concept notes in your table that identify the benefits and the costs described in the text. For example, you may decide that *economies of scale* is a benefit, in which case, you should write *economies of scale* in the *Benefits* column.

There are no suggested answers for this activity because it is part of the preparation for your essay.

Comment

From your reading of Texts 5.1 and 5.2, you have identified several costs and benefits for multinational corporations in general. These give you a framework for reading the case study and identifying the costs and benefits of the Wal-Mart takeover of Asda.

Activity 5.11

Purpose: to frame the case study, identifying the costs and benefits of Wal-Mart's takeover of Asda.

Task: prepare a version of the completed costs and benefits table from Activity 5.10, which has space for adding new information from the case study. You could create two separate tables – one for benefits and one for costs. The important point is to use the key concept headings you identified in the previous activity.

Prepare another costs and benefits table which does not have the key concepts from Texts 5.1 and 5.2 but is blank except for the headings *Costs* and *Benefits*. This is for information in the case study which does not fit into the categories in your framework but which is obviously a cost or a benefit of the takeover. If you find information like this in the case study, create a new key concept for it in the blank costs and benefits table.

Using costs and benefits tables and any other note-making method that you think will be successful, re-read the case study, making notes of data, explanations or claims that you can use in your essay on the costs and benefits of the Wal-Mart takeover of Asda takeover.

Save these notes as you will need to refer to them throughout the writing process.

There are no suggested answers for this activity because it is part of the preparation for your essay.

5.6 Writing the essay

The information in the frameworks you created during the last two reading activities will form the basis of your essay. However, the information is not yet organised into an essay outline format. In this section, you will organise it, first, into a key concept outline and then into a point-based outline. Finally, you will write a first draft of the essay.

Before the next activity, look at Activity 2.19 in Session 2, which gives examples of a concept-based and a point-based outline.

Activity 5.12 ....

Purpose: to produce a concept-based and a point-based essay outline.

Task 1: this activity builds on the analysis of the assignment title you did in Activity 5.2, the essay design work you did in Activity 5.3 and the questions you created in Activity 5.4.

Using the tables of concepts you created in Activities 5.10 and 5.11 and the essay design you created in Activity 5.3 as a basis, design a concept-based outline for an essay that answers the question in the assignment title.

Task 2: look at the criteria in Section B of the essay-writing checklist and develop the concept-based outline into a point-based outline. Think about what your argument is. Think about what claims you will make, how you will explain these claims, and what evidence you have for them from the case study.

Save these outlines because you will need to refer to them while writing the essay.

There are no suggested answers for this activity because it is part of the preparation for your essay.

In the next activity, you write a first draft of the essay. This should be based on the texts you have read in this session and the frameworks, outlines and mind maps you have made. For this draft, you should not attempt to read any other texts than those you have already read. As you write the draft, refer to Sections A, B and C of the essay-writing checklist to remind you of the criteria that will be used to assess your essay.

Activity 5.13 ....

Purpose: to write a first draft of the essay.

Task: write a first draft of the essay with the title given in eTMA 03.

Guidance

Refer to the texts you have read, the notes and outlines you have produced, and the essay-writing checklist. Produce the draft in any way you like, but remember it is only a first draft and not the finished product. You should not expect it to be ready to give to your tutor at the end of this process. After producing this first draft you still have another two weeks to work on the assignment.

As you write the draft, try out some of the essay-writing skills and features introduced in this book. They are summarised in the essay-writing checklist. You should save the draft, as it will be used in the assessment of your essay.

There are no suggested answers for this activity because it is part of the assignment you will be assessed on.

5.7　Review

This session took you up to the first draft stage of writing a 'costs and benefits' essay on a multinational takeover. In the process, you should have developed your vocabulary for discussing multinational corporations, takeovers, and costs and benefits. You should have applied and developed all the reading, note-making and essay-outlining skills you have practised during the course so far. You have designed a critical discussion essay both in outline form and in first draft form during which you have applied the argument-structuring skills introduced in the course. Throughout, you have referred to the essay-writing checklist of the criteria for a successful essay, which will be used in the assessment of your assignment. This first draft now provides the basis of the activities you will do in the final session of this book.

5.8　Critical reflection

- Have you changed any of the procedures suggested in the activities in this session to suit your own essay-writing style?
- Do you think academic writing style is unnecessarily complicated? If so, why?
- What is the most valuable thing you have learned about essay writing in this session?
- What do you still need to learn about essay writing?

Use the online Learning Journal for your personal reflection.

5.9 Answer section

Activity 5.1

This activity is a reminder that producing an essay is a process. You might start thinking about:

1 the processes that **you** would use to produce this essay – even if some of the procedures you are later asked to carry out in Sessions 5 and 6 are different from what you might choose to do

2 what you know about this area of business studies and which business studies texts might be useful – even if they are not exactly the ones you are asked to read

3 the design of the final essay – even though this will probably go through many changes before it is finished.

Activity 5.2

Task 1

The tasks and knowledge indicated by the assignment title include at least the following.

What does the title expect me to do?	What key concepts does the title expect me to deal with?
Critically discuss Focus on costs and benefits	See the mind map in Figure 5.7. This is a simple mind map based on the most obvious concepts in the title and in the notes. You could develop a far more complex one with more knowledge about the subject of the title.

Tasks 2 and 3

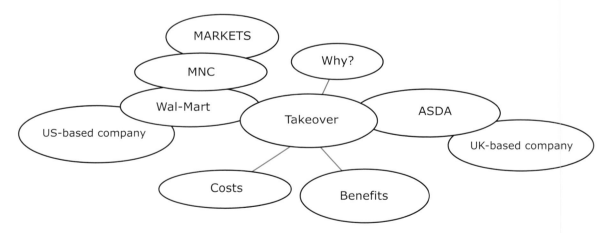

Figure 5.7   Mind map for answer to Activity 5.2

Activity 5.3

Task 1

Costs	Benefits
destroy, bring in, repatriate profits, pose problems, increase uncertainty, insecurity	stimulate, bring, raise, induce, promote

Task 2

Generally, costs language is negative and benefits language is positive. Typical negative costs words are *destroy*, *pose problems* and *increase uncertainty*. Typical positive benefits words are *bring benefits*, *stimulate* and *promote*. So the paragraph about the costs for developing countries has these negative words. However, the costs paragraph also has positive words because it includes information about the advantages that a multinational company has in a developing country. The paragraph has positive words for the *benefits* the company has, even though these advantages are not positive for the developing country – in fact, they are *costs*.

Task 3

(a)   Domestic rivals, and supporting and complementary industries.

(b)   The main cause is MNC investment but this leads to other causes, including new technologies and managerial competencies.

(c)   Inter-firm competition.

(d)   Transportation companies are supporting; packaging companies are complementary.

(e)   See Figure 5.8.

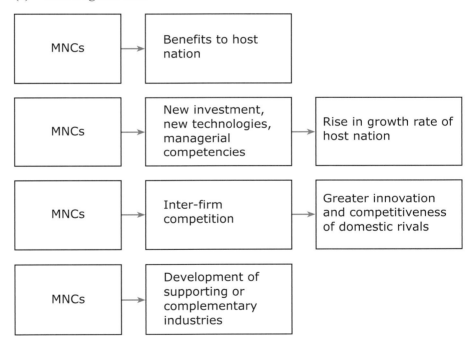

Figure 5.8   Answer to Activity 5.3, question (e)

(f)   MNCs can create problems for developing countries.

(g)   MNCs have such a competitive advantage over local firms.

(h)   MNCs obtain their components from abroad.

(i)   MNCs bring most of their profits back to their home country.

(j)   MNCs can relocate at any time.

(k)   Sourcing of materials from abroad; repatriation of profits; ability to relocate.

Activity 5.5

Some of the texts are more obviously useful than others but, to some extent, the ordering is a personal preference. The following order is not the only possible order: 1 (g); 2 (a); 3 (h); 4 (f); 5 (e); 6 (b); 7 (c); 8 (d).

Activity 5.7

Task 1: Reading

1   No suggested answer because it is individual to you.

2   Introduction; definition; reasons; problems.

3   No suggested answer.

4   They do not own foreign assets.

5   The following is an example. The term 'ownership pattern' refers to the relationship between the parent company and its subsidiary companies in other countries. Either the parent company can own the subsidiaries completely, or there can be a shared ownership which is known as a 'joint venture'.

6   Both turnover and GDP refer to the total value of goods and services. In the case of turnover, it refers to the value of goods and services sold by a company during a particular period of time. In the case of GDP, it refers to the total value of goods and services produced within a country in a year. Many multinational companies have a higher turnover than some small countries.

7   The reason why going multinational could lead to a reduction in costs is that going multinational can provide access to cheaper resources such as labour or raw materials, or reduce the need to transport goods or materials long distances.

8   Exploiting an advantage over a rival is probably **both** a cause **and** an effect of growth. It could be the reason why a company goes multinational – by moving into a new country in order to exploit its advantages. It could also be the result of going multinational – as a result of moving into a new country, a multinational can exploit its advantages.

9   Interest is an example of a fixed cost. Interest is the money that a company pays for borrowing money. By borrowing money in order to expand its operations, a multinational may increase its output so much that, when the fixed cost of the borrowing is compared with the increased output, the fixed cost per unit of output is reduced. This is a result of *economies of scale*.

10 A company producing cars might want to sell these cars in another country where there are restrictions on the importation of foreign cars. As a result, the car-producing company might try to take over a car company in the country with the import restrictions.

11 The problems can be paired as follows, although this doesn't mean that the two problems in a pair have exactly the same meaning – they are just related to similar aspects of going multinational. 1 *Problems relating to operating in a new and unfamiliar environment* and *cross-cultural issues*. 2 *Coordination of the activity of subsidiaries located in different parts of the world* and *diseconomies of scale*.

Task 2: Language focus – word combinations

ownership of	foreign assets
ownership of	productive assets
ownership of	superior technology
ownership of	managerial expertise
productive	assets
foreign	assets
to export	goods or services
to have	a turnover that exceeds £100 billion
reduction	in costs
to spread	costs
fixed	costs
labour	costs
transport	costs
costs	of raw materials
exploit	a competitive advantage
exploit	economies of scale
suffer	diseconomies of scale
locate	operations
jump	tariff barriers
circumvent	import restrictions

Activity 5.8

Task 1

1 Introduction – opening three paragraphs; definition – What is a multinational corporation?; reasons – Why do businesses go multinational?; problems – problems facing multinationals.

   Aspects not covered by Text 5.1 – MNCs and the UK economy.

2 No, the information about size at the end of paragraph 1 in Text 5.1 comes from several different parts of the first section of Text 5.2.

3 Overseas business relative to total business; production locations.

4 It does not represent the great variety of MNCs.

5   *foreign subsidiary*

6   *business activity*

7   *national income*

8   There is no such thing as a **typical** MNC business.

9   MNCs locate to areas where the resources available meet the MNC's particular resource needs.

10   To share risk or because governments insist that they do.

11   *subservient*

12   The main company in an MNC can have different relationships with its foreign productive assets. Either foreign companies can be completely controlled by the main company, or the foreign companies can be independent, but joined to the main company by a group of shared goals.

The style of this paraphrase is reasonably academic. This is partly because some business studies terms from other parts of the source text have been used: for example, *foreign productive asset* for *overseas or international subsidiary*. However, there are several business studies terms in the source text which would be better than the ones used here: *parent company* for *main company*; *organisational form* for *relationship*; *dominant* and *subservient* for *completely controlled*; *set of global objectives* for *group of shared goals*. This shows that, when paraphrasing, you need to decide whether some of the words in the original source text are actually necessary for communicating effectively. At the same time, you need to ensure that you are not copying so many original words that you plagiarise the text.

Task 2

1   The point is to emphasise the high level of MNC investment in the UK.

2   A horizontally integrated multinational is an MNC that produces virtually the same product in all the countries where it is located. Its purpose is to grow through expansion into different markets.

A vertically integrated multinational deals with different parts of its production process in different countries. In some countries it will concentrate on the upstream processes and in other countries the downstream ones. Companies do this in order to control costs and manage environmental uncertainty. Examples of this kind of MNC are oil companies including Shell and Exxon.

A conglomerate multinational diversifies production across different countries. It does this to manage risk through the careful purchase of overseas assets. An example of this kind of MNC is Hanson Corporation.

3   MNCs can be divided into those that are using their multinational base primarily as a means of achieving growth [*horizontal and conglomerate multinationals*] and those that are using it to reduce costs [*vertically integrated multinationals*].

4   The answer to the question in the title depends on the kind of MNC which is being considered.

Task 3

1   Labour, capital and raw materials.

2   MNCs locate where factors of production are available. Labour is one of these factors. If labour is available, and if the relative cost of that labour is low, an MNC may move to this low cost labour location. An example of this is Nike's movement of its production operations to developing countries.

3   Nike organises its production globally by taking advantage of cost conditions. It has outsourced all its production processes to countries where production costs are low. If production costs, mostly wages, in any of these countries rise, Nike can move production to other countries where costs are lower. The most important information for managing this arrangement is information about changes in cost conditions internationally.

4   One of the reasons why so many multinational companies invest in the UK is the factor quality of labour in the UK. Although labour costs are reasonably high, the labour quality is also high. This means that labour costs per unit of output make the UK attractive to multinational investors (Sloman and Sutcliffe, 2000, p. 201).

5   Going multinational reduces transport costs by bringing production assets closer to raw materials, resources or markets and thus reducing the length of the journey from production asset to suppliers or markets.

Key concepts: *production assets, raw materials, resources, suppliers, markets.*

Paraphrased: *overseas plants = production assets; bringing production assets closer = locating production; local raw materials = suppliers, resources.*

6   *avoidance of tariffs*

7   Attract inward investment.

8   The provision of premises reduces MNCs' fixed costs of rent or property purchase, increases economies of scale, and thus improves the investment risk.

Task 4

1   The two general effects of becoming multinational are: to spread a company's risks; to exploit any specific advantages over foreign rivals in their home market.

Both word combinations are particularly effective and it would be reasonable to use them as they are in the source text.

2   Ownership of superior technology; entrepreneurial and managerial skills; research and development capacity. Again these are useful word combinations and it is difficult to provide better alternatives.

3   Ownership of superior technology improves productivity levels and product quality.

Managerial skills can lead to superior efficiency and productivity.

Because they can afford high levels of investment in R&D, MNCs lead the world in process innovation and product development.

Task 5

1   In the launch phase, the novelty of the product leads to high profits.

In the growth phase, falling prices mean the company thinks about moving production to low-cost countries.

In the mature phase, saturated markets encourage the company to develop overseas markets and also reduce costs by moving production there.

When original markets go into decline, MNCs focus on markets in developing countries and move production to even lower-cost countries.

2   Being able to move production assets to new locations lowers costs and makes it possible to continue generating profits after a product would have become unprofitable if its production had continued in its original location.

Task 6

1   The text implies that in developing countries fewer local people are employed – perhaps because the skills they have differ from those needed to work for the MNC.

2   Cultural insensitivity

3   Interventionist

4   When communication lines are long and complex, and parent companies seek to exercise a high level of control over subsidiaries, diseconomies of scale are more likely than when parent companies are less controlling.

SESSION 6 Quality control in essay writing

6.1 Introduction

By working through Session 5, you have already made good progress towards preparing the essay which is the assessed assignment for this part of the course.

You have developed the vocabulary necessary for discussing the key concepts of the essay. You have read and made notes on two input texts and applied them to the case study. You have considered the design, drawn up an outline, and written a first draft. Throughout this process you have referred to the essay-writing checklist of the criteria for a successful essay, which will be used to assess your assignment. Your first draft will provide the basis for the activities you will do in this final session of Book 2.

However, the range of source materials you have used so far has been very limited. In this session you will read several more texts which will contribute to the development of your argument. You will then work towards integrating these new ideas and perspectives in a final version of your essay. This corresponds to the output box of the production process introduced earlier in this book (Figure 6.1).

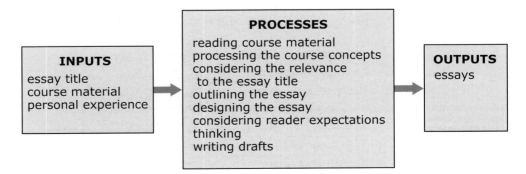

Figure 6.1 Producing an essay

Learning outcomes

In this session, you will:

- review the essay-writing checklist
- continue your reading of input texts for your essay
- draft and redraft the content, organisation and style of your work
- edit the grammar of your essay and check its presentation
- practise quoting, reporting and referencing
- create a customised version of the essay-writing checklist.

6.2 The essay-writing checklist

You have already encountered the first three sections of the checklist of features of a successful business studies essay, namely:

A   Use of source materials (Sessions 2 and 3)

B   Structure and development of text (Sessions 3 and 4)

C   Control of academic writing style (Sessions 4 and 5).

In this session you review your work against the criteria in Sections A, B and C. You will also draw on the final two sections of the checklist: D 'Grammatical correctness' and E 'Qualities of presentation'.

Section D includes the following features of a successful essay:

1   clause structure follows recognisable and appropriate patterns of English

2   correct subject–verb agreement

3   consistent and appropriate choice of tense, correctly formed

4   correct singular/plural noun agreement.

Session 1 introduced clause structure and correct subject–verb agreement.

Section E of the checklist covers the following features:

1   generally correct spelling

2   appropriate word processing

3   paragraphing reflects essay structure

4   capitals, italics, etc.

The full checklist is in the Appendix at the end of this book.

Reflecting on your essay writing

Activity 6.1   ....

Purpose: To reflect on aspects of your essay writing.

Task 1: you wrote a draft essay at the end of Session 2 and another one at the end of Session 5. Now consider the following questions.

1   What do you do well in essay writing?

2   What areas do you have difficulty with? Make a list of your strengths and another of your weaknesses.

3   Are your perceptions of your strengths and weaknesses the same as or different from the views of your tutor or other people who have commented on your work?

4   What areas have you improved on since you started this course? What do you still find challenging?

5   Are there any sections or specific criteria in the essay-writing checklist that you find particularly straightforward, or especially difficult?

Task 2: drawing on your observations in Task 1, write two or three paragraphs about your strengths and weaknesses in your essay writing. When you have finished, save the text in your Learning Journal.

Your answers are individual to you, so there is no feedback for this activity. However, keep a copy of your essay to hand as you will need to refer to it again later in this session.

Comment ....

You may be very clear about the areas you want to focus on to produce more successful essays. Alternatively, you may be able to specify some area but be less sure exactly how to describe others.

You can learn a lot from focusing on the strengths and weaknesses of other people's writing. This course contains many examples of students' writing for this purpose.

6.3 Developing your essay

This book has underlined the fact that the essay-writing process is a dynamic one during which your level of understanding and views about a particular subject area evolve through reading and reflection.

Writing the first draft of your essay is a significant point in this process in its attempt to bring your existing knowledge and perspectives together and present them in the form of a coherent argument.

Yet this is only the beginning. You will now read two more input texts. These will give another perspective on your essay. Later you will be directed to a selection of web-based sources, which will contribute further to the development of your ideas and understanding.

You will then need to return to your first draft and incorporate this new content into your argument. The process of reworking your text is called **redrafting**. It is perhaps the most important stage in the production of your essay. Your final task will be to edit your work. This concerns the grammatical and presentational aspects of your essay. Once you have completed this, your essay will be ready to be submitted.

6.4 Reframing your essay

The reading and preparation that you did in Session 5 looked at Wal-Mart's takeover of Asda primarily from the perspective of the costs and benefits to both companies. This focus framed your reading, note making, outlining and writing so far.

This section introduces two additional texts. These discuss the costs and benefits of a company takeover to the host nations that are affected. These theoretical source texts are, in fact, further extracts of the source materials in Session 5:

Text 6.1: Suneja, V. (2000) *Understanding Business Behaviour, Markets, Module 2 Study Guide*, The Open University, Milton Keynes.

Text 6.2: Sloman, J. and Sutcliffe, M. (2000) 'Multinational corporations', in Suneja, V. (ed.) *Understanding Business: Markets*, London, Routledge, pp. 196–212.

As mentioned in Session 5, Text 6.1 is an introductory text, giving an overview of the potential costs and benefits to the host countries involved. Text 6.2 is a more complex academic text which develops this discussion in more detail. You briefly considered two paragraphs from Text 6.1 in Activity 5.3. These focused specifically on the impact of a company takeover on **developing countries**. Your reading in Session 2 explored similar issues. As you will see, this is only one aspect of Texts 6.1 and 6.2.

Before starting to read, spend a few minutes considering what some of the costs and benefits of a company takeover might be to the countries involved.

Think back to the mind map and the concept-based outline that you devised in Session 5. Their main focus was probably on the costs and benefits of a takeover to Wal-Mart and Asda. How could they be developed to account for the perspective of the host nation involved in this instance – namely, the UK?

Activity 6.2 ....

Purpose: to develop your original mind map and concept outline to accommodate a new perspective.

Task: look back at the mind map and concept-based outline you created in Activity 5.2 and Activity 5.12.

How might you develop either of them so that they include the additional perspective of costs and benefits to host nations?

Within this new framework, brainstorm any questions, consider the possible answers and add any other ideas that you want to explore about the additional perspective to your essay.

There is no suggested answer for this activity because your framework, questions and ideas are individual to you.

Checkout tills at an Asda Wal-Mart store

Language work: word combinations

As you saw in Session 5, studying business is partly a process of learning what words go together best in order to communicate about business. This is the aspect of communication referred to in criterion C4 of the essay-writing checklist: *appropriate combinations of words*. Texts 6.1 and 6.2 contain many examples of word combinations. This next activity focuses on a sample of those associated with the costs and benefits of a company takeover to the host country.

Activity 6.3 ....

Purpose: to identify the word combinations that are associated with a particular area of business studies.

Task 1: complete the following sentence by matching each verb in the left-hand column below with a noun group in the right-hand column. Some of the verbs can be used more than once.

With respect to the host country, one of the effects of an MNC's takeover of a local company is to:

	Verb	*Noun group*
1	attract	economic uncertainty
2	stimulate	tax revenues
3	destroy	local incomes and expenditure
4	improve	the country's development priorities
5	distort	the development of supporting industries
6	increase	the country's balance of payments
		local competition
		further investment

Task 2: which of the combinations that you have identified have positive meanings, and are therefore considered **benefits**? Which of the combinations have negative meanings, and are therefore considered **costs**? Which verb carries both these meanings?

Task 3: the matching activity that you did in Task 1 involves the combination of a verb + a noun phrase. As mentioned throughout this course, academic writing uses a high number of **nouns**.

Thus, instead of using a verb, as in the following sentence:

1   *A positive effect of an MNC's takeover of a local company is that very often it <u>attracts</u> further investment into the host country.*

the preference is to use a noun:

2(a) One of the effects of an MNC's takeover of a local company is <u>the</u> <u>attraction of</u> further investment into the host country.

or

2(b) <u>The attraction of further investment</u> may be considered another benefit of an MNC's takeover of a local company.

Write five sentences to describe either the costs or the benefits of an MNC's takeover of a local company, by converting verbs 2 to 6 in the table in Task 1 into noun forms. Note that not all verbs change their form when converted into nouns. However, as nouns, they are all followed by a **preposition** such as *of* or *in*.

Try to vary the sentence structures, by placing the nouns in different positions, as in examples 2(a) and 2(b) above. Try also to use *the* before some nouns and *a* or *an* before others.

Compare your answers with those suggested in the Answer section.

Reading and note making

Texts 6.1 and 6.2 in Resource Book 2 provide a new perspective for interpreting the essay title and framing the Asda Wal-Mart case study.

This next activity proposes a note-making format which enables you to combine the key concepts from each text within the same document and apply the resulting frame of analysis to the Asda Wal-Mart case study.

Activity 6.4   ....

Purpose: to read and make notes on two additional texts; to apply a new frame to your re-reading of the Asda Wal-Mart case study.

Preparation: for this note-making activity you need to use your word-processor to prepare a large grid on a landscape-format, A4-sized piece of paper, as in Figure 6.2.

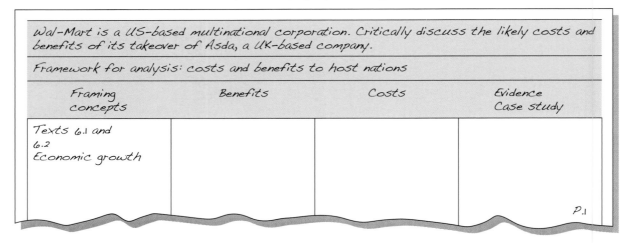

Figure 6.2   Example of a combinatory note-making format

Write the essay heading across the top of the grid, as shown. Below this, name the particular framework of analysis that is the focus of this reading of the source materials, as in the table.

In column 1 you should list the different framing concepts contained in the two academic source texts (Texts 6.1 and 6.2). One concept – *economic growth* – is provided as an example.

In column 2 you should make notes of any *benefits* to the host nations, starting with those associated with the concept of *economic growth*, as identified in your reading of the two texts. You should repeat this for *costs* in column 3.

When completed with your notes, columns 1–3 will provide a frame to apply to your re-reading of the Asda Wal-Mart case study.

Task 1: first, read Text 6.1 which introduces the main content areas of the more extensive academic text in Text 6.2. As you read, identify the key concepts framing the discussion of the costs and benefits for a country in which there is a company takeover and list them in column 1. As mentioned above, one key concept is given as an example. Use columns 2 and 3 to make notes on what the text identifies as benefits and costs to the host country as regards this key concept.

Task 2: now read Text 6.2 carefully and then answer the following questions.

How far does its content match the key concepts and notes that you have made in the grid so far?

What changes could you make to the organisation of the grid to accommodate the new content provided by Text 6.2? Take a few moments to reorder and re-label any key concepts in column 1 as required.

What additional information on costs and benefits does Text 6.2 contain that you think would usefully develop the notes you made on Text 6.1? Insert these additional notes into the costs and benefits columns as you work through the text. You could use an italic font to distinguish the new content from Text 6.2 from that of Text 6.1.

Task 3: now that you have identified the different concepts underpinning this new perspective on the essay title, the next step is to re-read the Asda Wal-Mart case study (Text 5.3 in Resource Book 2) with this new analytical frame in mind. As you do so, highlight and number any sections which you consider are relevant and insert the corresponding reference number in column 4 of your table.

There is no suggested answer for this activity because it is part of the preparation for your essay.

By drawing on a range of source materials, you can bring different voices, viewpoints and authoritative stances into your writing. This next section explains how to introduce such voices into your essay and how to ensure that the corresponding source texts are referenced correctly.

Language work: quoting, reporting and referencing

Quoting, reporting and referencing relate to criteria A4–A7 of the essay-writing checklist.

Quoting

Quoting is when you use the exact words that someone has said or written as support or evidence for the points that you make in your essay.

Below are examples from some student essays of quoting.

> According to Lucas, an economy is 'a system for the exchange of resources ... between the various stakeholders within the economy' (2000, p. 22).
>
> Nike's marketing strategy aims to 'integrate the swoosh into the cultural fabric of sports and harness its emotional power' (Sturges, 2005, p. 32).
>
> 'We've come around to saying that Nike is a marketing oriented company, and the product is our most important marketing tool', claims Phil Knight, the former CEO (quoted in Sturges, 2005).
>
> 'Eight thousand workers are employed there ...The ratio of women to men is seven to one. Most are migrant workers coming from all over China' (ARMC, 1997).

As these examples show, quoting follows particular conventions as follows.

- Quotations can be used for a single word, parts of a sentence or several sentences.

- The quoted words are normally enclosed within single quotation marks – ' '. In the case of a longer quotation consisting of three lines or more, the quotation marks should be omitted and the extract indented from the edge of the left-hand margin.

- Words should be quoted as they are in the source text and using the same punctuation. If, for reasons of clarity or simplicity, you leave a word or phrase out, this omission must be indicated with a sequence of three dots – ... – in place of the missing word or phrase. Similarly, if you add a word of your own to a quotation, this needs to be indicated by putting it in square brackets – [ ].

- All quotations should be accompanied by an in-text reference (see below), indicating precisely where they have come from.

Reporting

Unlike quotations, which use a person's exact words, reporting uses a form of paraphrase to refer to their words or ideas, as in the following student examples.

> With a market share of 45% in the USA and 35% in the UK (Sturges, 2005, p. 11), Nike is currently the world's biggest training shoe company.
>
> The circular flow of income model can be used to analyse the potential impact of a corporation on the economy of a developing country by illustrating the relationship between businesses and other economic agents (Coates, 1991).
>
> With reference to China, Junne (1995) warns that, without government intervention, tensions may arise between local economies.

As with quotations, all reported words and ideas should be accompanied by an in-text reference (see below) to indicate their source.

Referencing

Although you will have noticed and perhaps already used referencing techniques during this course, this criterion in Section A of the checklist has not been considered in detail so far.

There are two parts to the referencing process: **in-text referencing** and **making a list of references**.

In-text referencing

In-text references are incorporated into the essay. They need to be used each time you include someone else's ideas in your writing, whether you do this by summarising, paraphrasing, quoting or reporting.

Look back at the extracts from students' writing. They all include in-text references. As you can see, in-text references give the author's surname, the date of publication and, optionally, the page number of the source text in brackets. The full details are included in the list of references or bibliography at the end of the essay.

List of references

This is a detailed compilation of all the sources of information that you refer to in your essay. It should be under the heading 'References' or 'Bibliography' at the end of your essay. The list is normally presented in alphabetical order of the authors' surnames, as in the following example.

References

Coates, D. (2000) 'The management of the UK economy', in Lucas M. (ed.) *Understanding Business: Environments*, Routledge, London, pp. 55–70.

Dosi, G. (1988), 'Sources, procedures and micro-economic effects of innovation', *Journal of Economic Literature*, vol. 25, pp. 1120–71.

Lucas, M. (2000) *Environments. Module 1 Study Guide*, The Open University Business School, Milton Keynes,

Richardson, B. (2005) BBC News, Adidas bid raises image concerns, http://newsvote.bbc.co.uk/mpapps/pagetools/print/news. bbc.co.uk/2/hi/business/4741 [accessed 15 November 2005].

Sloman, J. and Sutcliffe, M. (1998) 'When markets fail', in Suneja, V. (ed.) (2000) *Understanding Business: Markets*, Routledge, London, pp. 117–44.

Sturges, J. (2000) 'Keep on running: the training shoe business', The Open University Business School, Milton Keynes.

Suneja, V. (2000) *Understanding Business Behaviour: Markets. Module 2 Study Guide*, The Open University, Milton Keynes.

Vanderbilt, T. (1998) *The Sneaker Book: Anatomy of an Industry and an Icon*, The New Press, New York, NY.

There are several different acceptable formats for presenting in-text references and lists of references. They generally contain the same kind of information but vary in how this is ordered and punctuated. Individual institutions very often stipulate which format they prefer. The one outlined here is called the **Harvard system**. (The origin of Harvard referencing is attributed to the cataloguing system used by the library of Harvard's Museum of Comparative Zoology.) Whichever format you use, it is important to follow its conventions – whether for entire books, book chapters, journal articles or web pages – carefully and systematically.

Activity 6.5   ....

Purpose: to note the Harvard formatting rules for documents in a list of references.

Task 1: look back at the list of references above. Identify and label each one according to whether it is:

- a book or a complete publication
- a chapter from a book
- a journal article
- a web page.

Task 2: match each type of document against one of the following four formats. Write out which is which against the numbers 1 to 4 below.

1 _____

Author's surname	,	Initial(s)	,	Year of publication	,	Title of work in inverted commas	,	Title of journal italicised or underlined	Volume no.	:	Page nos

2 _____

Author's surname	,	Initial(s)	Year of publication in brackets	,	Title of work italicised or underlined	.	Publisher	:	Place of publication

3 _____

Author's surname or institution	,	Initial(s)	Year of publication in brackets	Title of work italicised or underlined	,	Website address underlined	,	Date accessed in square brackets

4 _____

Author's surname	,	Initial(s)	,	Year of publication in brackets	,	Title of work in inverted commas	,	in	Author's surname	,	Initial(s)	Title of work	:	Page nos

Additional notes

(a) Where two or more authors are associated with a particular publication, they are listed as in the reference to Sloman and Sutcliffe above.

(b) If a work appears as a chapter in a book, the book itself should be included as a separate entry in the reference list. An example of this is the book by Suneja which contains the chapter by Sloman and Sutcliffe.

(c)   For edited collections, you should add (ed.) or (eds) after the editor(s), as in the book by Suneja.

There is further information on the Harvard referencing system in the Student Toolkit *The Effective Use of English*, which is available from the Open University's StudentHome page.

Activity 6.6 ....

Purpose: to practise writing a list of references.

Task: organise the following source information into a reference list, presenting it correctly in the Harvard style.

- A book called Mirages and Miracles: The Crisis of Global Capitalism, published in 1987 in London by Verso and written by A. Lipietz.
- An article called Divisions over the international divisions of labour, written by R. Jenkins in 1987 and corresponding to pages 28–57 of volume 2 of a journal called Capital and Class.
- A book called The New International Division of Labour, written by F. Frobel, J. Heinrichs and O. Drey and published by Cambridge University Press in New York in 1980.
- A chapter called Globalisation or Rival Trade Blocs, written by G. Junne in 1995, corresponding to pages 81–89 of Understanding Business: Environments, published by Routledge in London and edited by M. Lucas.
- A web page by Biz/ed called The Causes of Inflation, retrieved from www.bize.ac.uk/virtual/dc/copper/theory/th17.htm on January 21 2007.

Compare your answers with those suggested in the Answer section.

6.5   Editing your work

Editing involves the quality control checks that are needed in the final stages of essay writing. Editing should be done from two main perspectives: **grammatical correctness** and **quality of presentation**, which are considered further below.

Grammatical correctness

Section D of the essay-writing checklist addresses grammatical correctness. This concerns the appropriate construction of sentences, agreement between nouns and verbs and other aspects of using language correctly:

D1   clause structure follows recognisable and appropriate patterns of English

D2   correct subject–verb agreement

D3   consistent and appropriate choice of tense, correctly formed

D4   correct singular/plural noun agreement.

It is not possible to consider here all the grammatical problems that might occur in essay writing. Instead the discussion is limited to two very frequent problems in students' essays: **run-on** and **incomplete sentences** and **singular/plural noun agreement**.

Run-on sentences and incomplete sentences

Run-on sentences are sentences that should be broken up by full stops into shorter sentences, with full stops in between. Instead they continue into the next sentence and perhaps the one beyond, often with only commas separating them.

Incomplete sentences are the opposite. These sentence fragments sound odd when read independently of the sentences before or after them, as part of them is missing. They can often be corrected by creating a link between them and the sentence preceding or following them.

Activity 6.7

....

Purpose: to identify and rewrite run-on and incomplete sentences.

Task: read the extracts from students' writing below. Identify which contain run-on sentences (R) and which contain incomplete sentences (I). Then rewrite them so they are grammatically more correct.

> (a) There are three key reasons for the success of Nike, the first of these is their production and manufacturing policy.
>
> (b) Many definitions of a multinational company exist, a simple description is '*a business that either owns or controls foreign subsidiaries in more than one country*' (Sloman and Sutcliffe, 2000). The important feature being this control or ownership, as opposed to simply operating in these countries.
>
> (c) By diversifying their advertising and building relationships with customers of all ages and all fitness levels. They build on people's dreams of being the next Michael Jordan or of achieving personal goals such as completing a marathon, all of this is possible, they claim, by wearing Nike.

Compare your answers with those suggested in the Answer section.

Singular/plural noun agreement

Look at the following extract from a student text. What is wrong with it? How might you correct it?

> The company believes that 'design is what makes a particular trainer stand out' (Sturges, 2000, p. 24). That is why they have employed more design personnel and increased their design budget.

The problem with this extract is that, in the first sentence, the word *company* is considered to be a singular noun and is used with the corresponding verb form: *the company believes*. Yet in the second sentence the pronoun *they* is used with the corresponding verb form *have*, followed by the pronoun *their* before the word *design*. (Traditionally pronouns such as *their*, *my*, etc. have also been called adjectives.)

This is a common problem when referring to companies or organisations as they can be considered either *singular* or *plural* entities. Both are acceptable but it is important to be consistent with using one or the other.

So, the above extract can be corrected to:

> The company believes that 'design is what makes a particular trainer stand out' (Sturges, 2000, p. 24). That is why it has employed more design personnel and increased its design budget.

or

> The company believe that 'design is what makes a particular trainer stand out' (Sturges, 2000, p. 24). That is why they have employed more design personnel and increased their design budget.

Which one do you prefer?

Activity 6.8 ....

Purpose: to identify and rewrite sentences containing incorrect singular/plural noun agreement.

Task: identify and correct the incorrect singular/plural noun agreements in the following extract.

> For a time Nike was not concerned with the ethical considerations of using cheap labour, as they did not consider this their responsibility. Nike now employ a vice-president for corporate and social responsibility (Sturges, p. 30). The role of this person is to ensure that the companies they outsource to are not exploiting their workers. Although this incurs extra costs for Nike, it will reap these back by being considered a responsible company and they can then use this as positive publicity.

Now check your answer with that suggested in the Answer section.

Qualities of presentation

Section E of the essay-writing checklist covers the *qualities of presentation*. Here the focus is on two of them: spelling (E1) and aspects of punctuation (E4).

E1   generally correct spelling

E2   appropriate word processing

E3   paragraphing reflects essay structure

E4   punctuation.

Spelling

English spelling can cause problems because it is not systematic. It is important to double-check any words that you are not sure about in a dictionary or a computer-based spell-checking facility. However, be careful with the latter as it is not foolproof.

It is much more efficient to learn to trust yourself rather than using a dictionary or spell-checker repeatedly with the same problematic words, particularly as sometimes neither resource will be available to you. Start keeping a list or booklet of words that you regularly misspell, alongside their correct equivalents. Focus in particular on words related to your field of study. Add other words as you encounter them.

Some people find it helps to invent memorable ways of recalling the spelling of particular words. Write out the word several times to remember it. Ask someone to test you by reading out several words at a time. Once you have written them out, check the words against the original. By doing this regularly you will soon master the spelling of these words and they will no longer be problematic for you.

The Student Toolkit *The Effective Use of English*, which is available from the OU StudentHome page at www.open.ac.uk/skillsforstudy/ students/sttktsc1_scr.pdf, contains further useful tips and information to help with your spelling.

Punctuation

Activity 6.9   ....

Purpose: to review the punctuation of a text.

Task: the punctuation and paragraphs are omitted from the following news article about Asda. Read it through once. Then, using the same text in the Resource Book (Text 6.3), correct the text, reinserting the punctuation and paragraphs as necessary.

i usually go to Tesco but i came here for the chicken mrs walmsley said standing near the poultry counter its a giveaway everything is going up in price so every day now we only eat chicken the chicken she was after was pale and not particularly appetising but one look at the label explained why she had made her special trip it weighed 1.5kg was British and fresh and cost just £2 mrs walmsleys most difficult choice was whether to buy two or three she took three asda and tesco are waging a price war and along with Harry Potter books and school uniforms chicken is on the frontline Asda boasts that its £2 chicken is now iconic one of the few foods that people will cross town for the miserable summer has more than made up for the loss of trade in barbecues, says rachel fellows a spokeswoman for the store the more people stay indoors the more they eat chicken it sometimes seems as though the super competitive stores are using chicken to snipe at each other just for the sake of it if Tesco reduces the price of its healthy frozen skinless chicken breast by a penny one week asda will follow suit the next i don't know how the supermarkets can sell it for £2 says Nigel Joice regional chairman of the national farmers unions poultry board who has invested millions of pounds to rear 880000 broiler chickens a year on a modern farm in north Norfolk he sells broiler eating chickens to most supermarket but declines to say which we are not losing money on the £2 bird fellows said the price works for the consumer and also the supplier who wants to sell large volumes but she adds they meet us part of the way which is asdas way of saying that the £2 chicken wars are driving down the prices paid to farmers

(Source: adapted from *The Guardian*, 2007)

Compare your answer with the one suggested in the Answer section.

Applying the essay-writing checklist

You now practise applying the complete essay-writing checklist to a sample of your work.

Activity 6.10

···

Purpose: to practise reviewing an assignment against the essay-writing checklist.

Preparation: you need to look at the essay you produced at the end of Session 2: *Discuss the extent to which a large corporation such as Nike might influence the economic health of a developing country.* If it is not available, you may use the assignment you wrote at the end of Book 1 instead.

You will need:

1 a copy of the **original version** that you sent to your tutor

2 a copy of the **tutor-marked version**, containing both the commentary on your text and any additional feedback on it.

Task 1: begin with the original version of your essay. With reference to Sections A–E of the essay-writing checklist, underline any areas which you think could be improved to make the essay more successful. Use a lettering and numbering system to match them against the sub-criteria in the checklist. It is not necessary to make changes to the original.

Task 2: now turn to the assessed version of the same essay and its accompanying notes. Read through your tutor's comments and feedback carefully.

- Did your tutor pick up on similar areas to those you identified in Task 1?
- Did your tutor miss some of these areas?
- Did your tutor include any additional observations?

There are no suggested answers to this activity because your answers are individual to you.

Creating a personalised version of the essay-writing checklist

Now that you have practised applying the essay-writing checklist and identified your particular strengths and weaknesses, it is time to create your own personalised version.

The intention here is not to replace the original checklist with an entirely new version. Rather, you should maintain the original version as a reference point, and write an adapted, supplementary version that is more suited to your specific requirements when redrafting and editing essays. This involves selecting the parts of its content that you consider most relevant, and adding any new items that you think are helpful.

Activity 6.11

···

Purpose: to draw up a personalised version of an essay-writing checklist.

Task: spend a few moments looking back at your observations on your essay writing in Activities 6.1 and 6.10.

Look at the complete essay-writing checklist in the Appendix. Read through each section in turn. Select the criteria that you think will be most useful to you in redrafting and editing your final assessed essay.

Are there any guidelines that are not in the original checklist that you want to add to your personalised version?

Now write out and organise these selected and new criteria in subsections in a personalised version of the checklist.

When you have finished, put a copy in MyStuff.

There is no suggested answer to this activity because it is part of the preparation for your essay.

6.6 Further reading

You now return to your draft essay again. You have read two new source texts in this session. This next section directs you to some additional input material which is on the internet.

The internet

Internet sources have been used for study purposes since the 1990s. They are often valuable in supplementing recommended sources of information. As with all source materials, it is important to take time to assess their relevance and reliability with respect to your work. For more information about using internet sources for your study, follow the links in 'Study support' from StudentHome.

Integrating text

Having read and made notes on a range of input texts and applied this as necessary to the Asda Wal-Mart case study, you now have a lot of new content with which to develop the essay.

The next step is to integrate this new information into the original draft essay which you wrote in Session 5. It is not sufficient simply to write another section and insert it into the first draft. Combining new content into the argument of an essay requires a reworking of the whole essay to ensure a seamless fit. This impacts on all three parts:

- the introduction
- the body
- the conclusion.

Bearing in mind the work that you did earlier on these three sections, consider the impact that incorporating a new section containing another perspective will have on the original design of your essay. What will you need to alter or revise? You consider this in the next activity.

Activity 6.12

Purpose: to anticipate the effects of adding new content to your original draft essay.

Task: in the table below, note down the broad changes or revisions that you need to make when integrating new material into the original design of your essay. Consider the impact on the introduction, the body and the conclusion. An example is given to get you started.

Compare your answers with those suggested in the Answer section.

Section	Changes needed
Introduction	Revise the central claim
Body	
Conclusion	

Writing a new essay outline

Activity 6.13

Purpose: to write a new outline for your essay.

Task 1: read through your sets of notes on the various input texts that you have processed in this session.

Task 2: now read through your original draft essay carefully, paying particular attention to its organisation and bearing in mind the new perspectives and ideas you reviewed in Activity 6.12.

Task 3: the next step is to design a revised **point-based** outline which incorporates this new content in your draft essay. You may prefer to begin with a concept-based outline to orient yourself, and then develop this into a point-based one, as you did in Activity 5.12.

6.7 Revising and redrafting your essay

Earlier in this session you were reminded that the essay-writing process is a dynamic one during which your views and understanding continue to evolve as you read and reflect on a particular subject area. You have assimilated a lot of new information since then and spent time considering how to integrate it into a more developed essay.

You are now at the point of returning to your first draft and rewriting it according to the new outline you devised in Activity 6.13. Yet you should not expect to create a final version in a single rewrite. Rather, you should allow for several redrafts as you continually evaluate and improve your essay. Re-reading a section, a moment's reflection or a flash of inspiration while away from your desk – any of these may suggest a new perspective or new connections or highlight inconsistencies in your work, causing you to revisit, develop and refine your argument. Such processes suggest that active learning is taking place as you continue to engage with the essay topic.

Activity 6.14 ....

Purpose: to redraft and edit your essay with reference to the essay-writing checklist.

Task: using your draft essay from Session 5 as a starting point, your new outline from Activity 6.13 for guidance, and your personalised essay-writing checklist as a point of reference, rewrite your essay, redrafting it as many times as necessary in the process. Your final task is to review the grammatical and presentational aspects of your essay, after which your essay will be ready to hand in.

Your tutor needs to see the changes in your essay from the first to the final draft, so you will need to submit:

- a copy of the two point-based essay outlines that contributed to the design of your essay (Activities 5.12 and 6.13).
- a copy of the draft essay you completed at the end of Session 5
- a copy of your final essay
- a copy of your personalised version of the essay-writing checklist.

6.8 Review

This final session of Book 2 brings together all the essay-writing processes that you have encountered in this book. You have processed a range of additional source material, revised your essay outline to accommodate new ideas and perspectives, and finished by redrafting and editing your essay using a personalised version of the essay-writing checklist.

6.9 Critical reflection

- Would you find it easier to write essays in a different style? What kind of style? Why?
- Why do you think universities ask students to write essays?
- Do you agree that essay writing is good preparation for professional communication in the workplace? In what ways is it similar? In what ways does it differ?

Use your online Learning Journal for your personal reflection.

6.10 Answer section

Activity 6.3

Tasks 1 and 2

	Verb	*Noun group*[*]
1	attract	further investment (B)
2	stimulate	local competition (B) the development of supporting industries (B)
3	destroy	local competition (C)
4	improve	the country's balance of payments (B)
5	distort	the country's development priorities (C)
6	increase (this verb has both meanings)	economic uncertainty (C) local incomes and expenditure (B) tax revenues (B) local competition (B)

* B = benefit; C = cost.

Task 3

Your sentences should contain the following nouns and prepositions: (the/a) stimulation of; (the/a) destruction of; (the/an) improvement in; (the/a) distortion of; (the/an) increase in.

Activity 6.5

Task 1

Book or complete publication: Lucas; Sturges; Suneja; Vanderbilt.

Chapter in a book: Coates; Sloman and Sutcliffe.

Journal article: Dosi.

Web page: Richardson.

Task 2

(1) Journal article; (2) book or complete publication; (3) web page; (4) chapter in a book.

Activity 6.6

Your list should be styled and arranged in order as follows.

Biz/ed (2006) 'The causes of inflation' [online], www.bize.ac.uk/virtual/dc/copper/theory/th17.htm (accessed 21 January 2007).

Frobel, F., Heinrichs, J. and Drey, O. (1980) *The New International Division of Labour*, Cambridge University Press, New York.

Jenkins, R. (1984) 'Divisions over the international divisions of labour', *Capital and Class*, vol. 2, pp. 28–57.

Junne, G. (1995) 'Globalisation or rival trade blocs', in Lucas, M. (ed.) *Understanding Business: Environments*, Routledge, London, pp. 81–89.

Lipietz, A. (1987) *Mirages and Miracles: The Crisis of Global Capitalism*, Verso, London.

Activity 6.7

(a)   There are three key reasons for the success of Nike (R). The first is their production and manufacturing policy.

(b)   There are many definitions of a multinational company (R). A simple description is 'a business that either owns or controls foreign subsidiaries in more than one country' (Sloman and Sutcliffe, 2000, p. 196), the important feature being this control or ownership, as opposed to simply operating in these countries (I).

(c)   By diversifying their advertising and building relationships with customers of all ages and all fitness levels (I), they build on people's dreams of being the next Michael Jordan or of achieving personal goals such as completing a marathon (R). All of this is possible, they claim, by wearing Nike.

Activity 6.8

For a time Nike was not concerned with the ethical considerations of using cheap labour, as **it did not** consider this its responsibility. Nike now **employs** a vice-president for corporate and social responsibility (Sturges, p. 30). The role of this person is to ensure that the companies it outsources to are not exploiting their workers. Although this incurs extra costs for Nike, it will reap these back by being considered a responsible company and **it can** then use this as positive publicity.

or

For a time Nike **were** not concerned with the ethical considerations of using cheap labour, as they did not consider this their responsibility. Nike now employ a vice-president for corporate and social responsibility (Sturges, p. 30). The role of this person is to ensure that the companies they outsource to are not exploiting their workers. Although this incurs extra costs for Nike, **they** will reap these back by being considered a responsible company and they can then use this as positive publicity.

Activity 6.9

'I usually go to Tesco, but I came here for the chicken,' Mrs Walmsley said, standing near the poultry counter. 'It's a giveaway. Everything is going up in price so every day now we only eat chicken.'

The chicken she was after was pale and not particularly appetising, but one look at the label explained why she had made her special trip. It weighed 1.5kg, was British and fresh, and cost just £2. Mrs Walmsley's most difficult choice was whether to buy two or three. She took three.

Asda and Tesco are waging a price war and, along with Harry Potter books and school uniforms, chicken is on the frontline.

Asda boasts that its £2 chicken is now 'iconic', one of the few foods that people will cross town for. 'The miserable summer has more than made up for the loss of trade in barbecues', says Rachel Fellows, a spokeswoman for the store. 'The more people stay indoors, the more they eat chicken.'

It sometimes seems as though the super-competitive stores are using chicken to snipe at each other just for the sake of it. If Tesco reduces the price of its healthy frozen skinless chicken breast by a penny one week, Asda will follow suit the next.

'I don't know how the supermarkets can sell it for £2,' says Nigel Joice, regional chairman of the National Farmers' Union's poultry board, who has invested millions of pounds to rear 880,000 broiler chickens a year on a modern farm in north Norfolk. He sells broiler (eating) chickens to most supermarkets, but declines to say which.

'We are not losing money on the £2 bird,' said Fellows. 'The price works for the consumer and also the supplier who wants to sell large volumes.' But, she adds: 'They meet us part of the way' – which is Asda's way of saying that the £2 chicken wars are driving down the prices paid to farmers.

Activity 6.12

Section	Changes needed
Introduction:	Revise the description of the essay outline Include more key concepts (it may be necessary to explain or define these)
Body:	Decide where to position any additional text Review the organisation of the body Use appropriate links and connecting words to introduce the new perspective(s) within the argument
Conclusion:	Adapt the link back to the title and to the essay's central claim Revise the summary of the argument Amend the reference to 'added value' and the final movement to a higher level as necessary

References

Clanchy, J., and Ballard, B. (1998) *How to Write Essays: a practical guide for students*, 3rd edition, South Melbourne, Australia, Addison-Wesley Longman.

The Guardian (2007) 'We bought this chicken in Asda this week ...', 4 August, [online] http://lifeandhealth.guardian.co.uk/food/story/0,,2141365,00.html [accessed 19 December 2007].

Giltrow, J. (1995) *Academic Writing*, Ontario, Canada, Broadview.

Oshima, A. and Hogue, A. (2006) *Writing Academic English*, New York, Pearson Education.

Sloman, J. and Sutcliffe, M. (1998) 'When markets fail', Chapter 7 in Suneja, V. (ed.) (2000) *Understanding Business: Markets*, London, Routledge, pp. 147–66. Reprinted from Sloman, J. and Sutcliffe, M. (1998) *Economics for Business*, London, Prentice-Hall Europe.

Sloman, J. and Sutcliffe, M. (2000) 'Multinational corporations', Chapter 10 in Suneja, V. (ed.) (2000) *Understanding Business: Markets*, London, Routledge, pp. 196–212.

Sloman, J. and Sutcliffe, M. (2001) *Economics for Business*, Harlow, Pearson Education Ltd, 2nd edition.

Suneja, V. (ed.) (2000) *Understanding Business: Markets*, London, Routledge.

Acknowledgements

Grateful acknowledgement is made to the following sources:

Text

Vidal, J. 'We bought this chicken in Asda this week. It cost £2 – the cheapest Europe has seen for decades. What does this new low mean for us, for poultry farmers, and for animal welfare?', *The Guardian*, August 4 2007, Guardian Newspapers Ltd.; pp. 105–6: Sloman, J. and Sutcliffe, M. (1998) *Economics for Business*, Pearson Education Ltd. © John Sloman and Mark Sutcliffe 1998, © Pearson Education 2001.

Figures/Ilustrations

Figure 3.3: Oshima, A., and Hogue, A., (2006) *Writing Academic English*, Pearson Education; page 14: © Huy Lam; page 40: © www.cartoonstock.com; page 43: © Jon Arnold Images/Alamy; page 59: © Chad Ehlers/Alamy; page 68: © www.cartoonstock.com; page 100: © Jon Arnold Images/Alamy; page 133: © Manor Photography/Alamy; page 149: © Getty Images/Photodisc; page 161: © Getty Images/Photodisc; page 164: © John Sturrock/Alamy; page 176: © Getty Images/Photodisc.

Appendix   Essay-writing checklist

Section A

Use of source material: is information from study and research correct and appropriate for the task?

Criteria

1   Relevant information from reading is used
2   Irrelevant information from reading is avoided
3   Information from reading or other research is interpreted correctly
4   Information from reading or other research is transferred correctly
5   Information is integrated with the text
6   Text is free from plagiarism
7   Bibliography or reference list is constructed correctly

Section B

Structure and development of the text: is the structure and development of the essay clear and appropriate to the title and its context?

Criteria

1   Text structure is appropriate to the task
2   Beginning of the essay introduces the argument
3   Beginnings of paragraphs and sentences orientate to the argument
4   Argument moves between high-level generalisations and low-level details and examples
5   Claims build up the argument
6   Evidence is used that supports the claims in the argument
7   Explanations link the evidence to the claims
8   Information flow in the argument is linked and connected
9   Statement of conclusion follows from argument and relates to title

Section C

Control of academic writing style: does the writing style conform to appropriate patterns of written academic English?

Criteria
1   Appropriate choice of vocabulary
2   Appropriate use of business concept words
3   Appropriate use of other abstract words
4   Appropriate combinations of words
5   Appropriate relationship with reader
6   Appropriate evaluation language

Section D

Grammatical correctness

Criteria
1   Clause structure follows recognisable and appropriate patterns of English
2   Correct subject–verb agreement
3   Consistent and appropriate choice of tense, correctly formed
4   Correct singular/plural noun agreement

Section E

Qualities of presentation

Criteria
1   Generally correct spelling
2   Appropriate word processing
3   Paragraphs reflect essay structure
4   Punctuation

(Source: adapted, with permission, from materials created by the MASUS Project, The University of Sydney, 1997.)

Index

Entries in **bold type** are defined in the course Glossary.